THE FLOUR POT

Christmas Cookie Book

✳ ✳ ❋ ✳ ✳

CREATING EDIBLE WORKS OF ART FOR THE HOLIDAYS

BY MARGIE AND ABBEY GREENBERG

Running Press
PHILADELPHIA · LONDON

TO FRED GREENBURG,
WITH LOVE

Library of Congress Control Number: 2009929428
ISBN 978-0-7624-3554-8

Book design by Amanda Richmond
Edited by Geoffrey Stone
Typography: Lomba & Futura

Running Press Book Publishers
2300 Chestnut Street
Philadelphia, PA 19103-4371

Visit us on the web!
www.runningpresscooks.com

✳ ❄ CONTENTS ❄ ✳

✳ ❉ ACKNOWLEDGEMENTS ❉ ✳

After we wrote our first book, *The Flour Pot Cookie Book*, we were flooded with emails from fans inspired by our decorative cookies asking when our second book was coming out. Delighted that people wanted more Flour Pot Cookie tips and designs, we forwarded some of the emails to our editor. And here we are. From the bottom of our hearts we thank you.

And of course, thank you to our family and friends, who inspire our holiday stories and traditions: Fred, Andy, Shiri, Hallie, Sara, Ira, Eva and the most recent addition to our family, Jake.

The dessert table is sweeter with you there.

✳ ❄ INTRODUCTION ❄ ✳

Abbey: From gingerbread house competitions to family cookie swaps, for as long as I can remember, the holiday season has been synonymous with cookies. For many people, the Christmas season is the only time they bake. Now owning a cookie company, I imagine if Santa's workshop has a Philadelphia outpost it would look like The Flour Pot in the month of December. This book is a collection of our most favorite and most creative holiday-themed cookies.

Margie: Sitting down to create cookies for this book was at first a daunting task. I had to put my creative thinking cap on. As I began to think about the holidays, I pulled all of my cookie cutters out on the table. Then it happened: I saw a Santa in a triangle shape; then a reindeer in a stocking shape. They were popping out of every cutter imaginable! So when you begin your baking, let your imagination run wild and don't ever take your cookie cutters at face value.

Abbey: Margie is always thinking out of the box. Sometimes I'm convinced she doesn't even believe a box ever existed! This book really is a tribute to that ability—to take pastry tips and use them as cookie cutters, or to take a gingerbread man cutter and turn him upside down to make a reindeer face. I am always amazed when a customer calls and asks for a specific design. Within a few seconds, Margie will figure out a way to

use what we have and repurpose it to get just what the customer ordered. We invite you to peruse through this book. But don't stop there. Look at the way we have made something, and imagine how you can put your own twist, your own personal touch, on your cookie. Think outside the box!

Margie: A plain cookie can become your canvas on which to use your creativity. Sometimes I think of cookies as a craft project using lots of imagination and candy accessories. I love the colors and varieties of shapes that you can find in the candy aisle of the supermarket. Start collecting cookie cutters! I have been collecting them for years. One of the benefits of having a huge assortment is that I can use parts of one cookie cutter to complete the look of another cookie.

✳ ❄ BASIC TOOLS ❄ ✳

- Rolling pin
- Cookie sheets
- Cookie cutters
- Fondant: For each 4-inch cookie, you need about 1 ounce of fondant
- Fondant rolling pin (plain and textured)
- Parchment paper
- Paintbrushes
- Corn syrup
- Pastry bags
- Pastry bag tips
- Colored gel paste
- Latex gloves
- Toothpicks
- Decorative accessories: candies, ribbons, sugar add-ons. We accessorize our cookies like some people accessorize with a scarf or belt. While plainly decorated cookies are pretty, we think they are oh so much prettier all decked out!

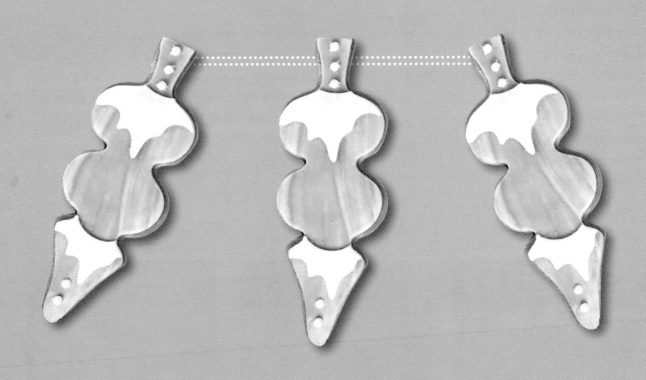

✳✳✳✳✳
WINTER CHILL
✳✳✳✳✳

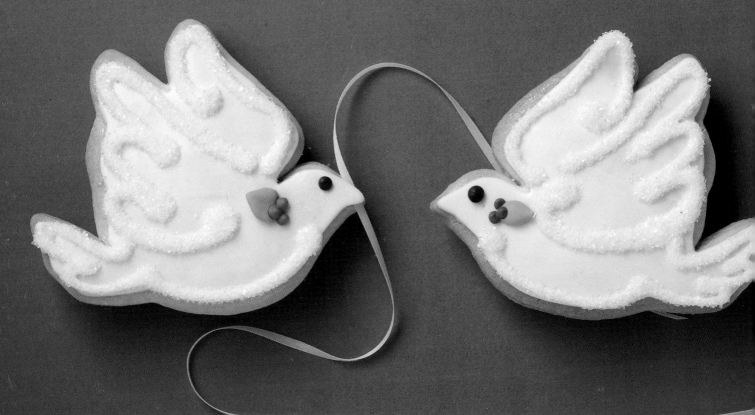

Peace Doves

Peace. What a wonderful sentiment for the holiday season!

✳ ✳ ❋ ✳ ✳

WHAT YOU NEED:

Parchment paper
Fondant rolling pin
White fondant
Dove cookie cutter
2 Paintbrushes
Corn syrup
Dove cookies
Super Pearl Luster Dust
Pastry bags with #2 tip
White royal icing
White sanding sugar
Red royal icing
Black royal icing
#352 Leaf tip
Green royal icing

DIRECTIONS:

On parchment paper, roll out the fondant to ⅛-inch thickness. Cut into dove shapes with your dove cookie cutter. Set aside.

With a paintbrush, dab the top of each cookie with corn syrup. Carefully place a fondant dove on top of the syrup, smoothing the edges with a dry finger. Use a dry paintbrush to cover the fondant with luster dust. Repeat for all of the cookies.

To decorate: Fill a pastry bag with a #2 tip with white royal icing. Pipe the wing detail and outline. Sprinkle with sanding sugar. Use red royal icing to finish the detail of the berries. Use black royal icing to create an eye. Using a pastry bag with a leaf tip, pipe the leaf, using green royal icing. Let dry for at least one hour or until the icing has hardened.

Tip: For more sugar coverage, put the sanding sugar in a small dish and dip each cookie in the sugar (sort of like dipping an ice cream cone into sprinkles). Shake off the excess.

Peekaboo Snowflakes

Abbey says: *I love the contrast of the dark background with the white icing. It makes the cutouts pop.*

WHAT YOU NEED:

Parchment paper

Fondant rolling pin

White fondant

Snowflake cookie cutter

2 Paintbrushes

Super Pearl Luster Dust

Assorted mini cookie cutters

Corn syrup

Chocolate snowflake cookie (see Chocolate Cookie Dough recipe, page 126)

Pastry bag with #2 tip

White royal icing

Dragées

DIRECTIONS:

Roll out the fondant on parchment paper to $\frac{1}{8}$-inch thickness. Cut into snowflake shapes with your snowflake cookie cutter. Use a dry paintbrush to dust each flake with luster dust.

Using mini cutters, cut into each snowflake in a random or symmetrical pattern. Set the cutouts aside.

With a paintbrush, very carefully dab corn syrup onto each cookie, being careful to moisten only the area that will be covered by fondant. Place the fondant snowflakes on top of the syrup, smoothing the edges with a dry finger.

To decorate: Fill the pastry bag with white royal icing. Use the icing to pipe the snowflake detail and to adhere a silver dragée to the center of each snowflake. Let dry for at least one hour or until the fondant is hardened.

Another idea: A gingerbread cookie would also work nicely here.

Tip: *When cutting details into the snowflake, be sure to leave enough fondant to adhere to the cookie with corn syrup.*

Icicles

Out of the box: Our icicle cookies create a wonderful, cool feeling for winter. Use a cool blue fondant color to give them a chilly icicle appearance. For the detail, use a cutter that has many pointed edges. We used a leaf cutter.

❄ ❄ ❄ ❄ ❄

WHAT YOU NEED:

Parchment paper
Fondant rolling pin
Blue fondant
Icicle cookie cutter
2 Paintbrushes
Corn syrup
Icicle cookie
White fondant
Maple leaf cutter
White royal icing
Pastry bag with #2 tip
Super Pearl Luster Dust
Sugar pearls
White sanding sugar
(optional)

DIRECTIONS:

Roll out the blue fondant on parchment paper to $\frac{1}{8}$-inch thickness. Cut into icicle shapes using your icicle cookie cutter. Set aside.

With a paintbrush, dab corn syrup on top of each cookie; then carefully place the fondant on top of the syrup, smoothing the edges with a dry finger. Set the prepared cookies aside.

To make the icy drip detail, roll the white fondant on parchment paper, as thin as you can. Cut with the leaf cutter. Use the icicle cutter to cut off the bottoms of each leaf so its edges match the cookie and it looks like icy drip.

Adhere the white fondant to the blue with white royal icing.

With a dry paintbrush, dust each cookie with luster dust.

Use dots of icing to adhere the sugar pearls.

While the icing is wet, sprinkle with sanding sugar for a touch of snow.

Let dry for at least one hour or until the royal icing is hardened.

Another idea: On your serving plate, lay the cookies on a pile of sanding sugar to add sparkle to the presentation. The sanding sugar looks like snow!

Tip: When layering fondant, make sure the second layer is thinner than the first.

Holly Leaves

*Margie says: This is a great cookie for decorators who don't love to pipe.
The interest in this cookie is really in the swirling of the fondant. I use lots of shades of
green and mix with white. I think the white adds a touch that looks like snow.*

✳ ✳ ❋ ✳ ✳

These cookies are great for leftover green fondant.

WHAT YOU NEED:

Green fondant

White fondant

Fondant rolling pin

Parchment paper

Holly Leaf cookie cutter

2 Paintbrushes

Corn syrup

Holly Leaf cookies

Toothpick

Super Pearl Luster Dust

Red royal icing

Pastry bag with #2 tip

White sanding sugar
(optional)

DIRECTIONS:

Combine green fondant (leftover, if you have it) with white to create a swirled effect. Do not incorporate the fondants completely; the more swirls, the better. Roll the mixed fondant on parchment paper to $\frac{1}{8}$-inch thickness. Cut it into leaf shapes with your Holly Leaf cookie cutter. Set aside.

With a paintbrush, dab corn syrup on top of each cookie. Next, carefully place a fondant leaf on the syrup, smoothing the edges with a dry finger. Repeat with all cookies. With a toothpick, create veins down the center and on the sides of the fondant. With a dry paintbrush, dust the fondant with luster dust. A little goes a long way. (Be careful to dust only the icing, not the cookie.)

With red royal icing in your pastry bag, pipe dots for the berries. While the icing is still wet, sprinkle a touch of white sanding sugar on the red berries.

Another idea: If you are looking for less of a Christmas look and more of a general, wintery look, substitute dark blue royal icing for the red royal icing.

Tip: When creating veins, press lightly with the toothpick. Be careful not to tear the fondant.

Scented Tree

Margie says: The spearmint leaf candy combined with fondant leaves adds a nice texture.

✳ ✳ ❄ ✳ ✳

WHAT YOU NEED:

Green fondant

White fondant

Fondant rolling pin

Parchment paper

Mini Leaf cookie cutter

2 Paintbrushes

Super Pearl Luster Dust

Jelly spearmint leaf candy

Tree cookie cutter

Corn syrup

Tree cookie

White royal icing

Pastry bags with #2 tip

Bow

White sanding sugar

Brown royal icing

Black royal icing

DIRECTIONS:

To create dimensional fondant leaves, combine green fondant with white fondant for swirled effect. Roll fondant on parchment paper to $\frac{1}{8}$-inch thickness. Cut into leaf shapes with your leaf cookie cutter. Dust the leaves with luster dust to add shimmer. Prop up the fondant leaves on a curved surface like a baking pan lip so they will dry in a curved shape. Let dry for at least one hour or until hard. These can be made a day or so ahead of time.

To create candy leaves, roll the jelly spearmint candy on parchment paper until paper thin, and cut with your leaf cookie cutter.

To create the tree, roll the swirled fondant on parchment paper to $\frac{1}{8}$-inch thickness. Cut it with your tree cookie cutter. Dab corn syrup on the top of each cookie. Place the fondant on the syrup, smoothing the edges with a dry finger.

To adhere the leaves, use white royal icing and start from the base of the tree working up. Intersperse fondant leaves with spearmint leaves, overlapping when necessary.

Pipe snow detail on the edges of the leaves. Sprinkle white sanding sugar on top of the icing to look like snow. Adhere the bow with white royal icing.

Using brown royal icing in a new pastry bag with a #2 tip, pipe the trunk detail. For contrast, pipe black royal icing over the brown trunk.

Tip: The spearmint leaves are a bit sticky to work with. Be careful lifting them off of the parchment, because you don't want them to tear.

SNOWY DAYS

Snow Babies

Margie says: Making clothes out of the fondant using the texture designs was lots of fun. What developed was less of a standard snowman, but a cookie that reminded me of a snow angel.

✳ ✳ ❋ ✳ ✳

WHAT YOU NEED:

Parchment paper
Fondant rolling pin
White fondant
Snowman cookie cutter
2 Paintbrushes
Corn syrup
Snowman cookie
Textured fondant
rolling sheets
Assorted cutters to
create outfits
Super Pearl Luster Dust
Pastry bag with #2 tip
White royal icing
White candy (optional
for buttons)
Black royal icing
Orange royal icing
Ribbon

DIRECTIONS:

Roll out the fondant on parchment paper to ⅛-inch thickness. Cut into snowmen with your snowman cookie cutter. Set aside.

With a paintbrush, dab corn syrup on top of each cookie; then carefully place a fondant snowman shape on top of the syrup, smoothing the edges with a dry finger. Set prepared cookies aside.

For snow baby clothes, roll a piece of white fondant on parchment paper to ⅛-inch thickness. Place a textured fondant sheet on parchment paper. Place the rolled fondant onto the textured sheet and roll over the fondant one time with your rolling pin to create the texture. Cut into snowman shapes with your snowman cutter. Then, using assorted cutters, make indents for the legs, neck, and arms of the outfit, and the hat. (*To create a wavy brim on the hat and a gentle ruffle on the dress, gently curl the bottom of the cap or dress with your finger.)

To assemble: Use a paintbrush to dab corn syrup on the tops of the prepared cookies. Carefully place the textured fondant garments on top of the syrup, smoothing the edges with a dry finger. Use a dry paintbrush to brush the entire fondant piece with luster dust.

To decorate: Pipe white royal icing from your pastry bag to add detail to the snow babies and their outfits. Also use white icing to adhere the white candy buttons to the fondant. Use orange royal icing in your pastry bag to pipe the nose, and black royal icing to pipe the eyes. (Optional: bows may be added with royal icing.)

Let the cookies sit for at least one hour or until the fondant is slightly hardened.

Sleds

Abbey says: My friend Jeremy lived through the woods from our house, on a big hill. After a snowstorm, my brothers and I would run over to Jeremy's house, and we would all race down the big hill on our sleds. After the fun, Jeremy's mom, Shelley, would have hot chocolate waiting for us.

✳ ✳ ❄ ✳ ✳

WHAT YOU NEED:

Parchment paper
Fondant rolling pin
White fondant
Textured rolling pin
Sled cookie cutter
1 Paintbrush
Corn syrup
Sled cookies
Offset spatula
Pastry bag with #2 tip
Red royal icing
White royal icing
Shoestring licorice
Candy canes

DIRECTIONS:

Roll white fondant on parchment paper to $\frac{1}{8}$-inch thickness. Go over the rolled fondant with a textured rolling pin until you get the imprints that you want.

Cut the fondant into sled shapes with your cookie cutter. Set aside.

With a paintbrush, dab corn syrup on top of each cookie. Carefully place a fondant sled on top of the syrup, smoothing the edges with a dry finger.

With an offset spatula, create five lines—or wood planks—down each sled. Make sure the edges of your spatula are clean. You may have to "rock" the spatula up and down to release the fondant. Be gentle.

Use red royal icing to decorate the borders of each sled. Let the icing dry.

Use white royal icing to adhere a piece of 6-inch licorice to the edge of each sled (one of the short sides). Let dry with the bottom of the sled facing up.

To assemble: Cover the candy canes with royal icing the length of the sled. (Only put icing on the candy canes where it will be concealed by the cookie.)

Adhere the cookie bottoms to the icing on the candy canes. Let dry.

Tip: Either a rounded rectangle cutter or a regular rectangle cutter is fine.

- **Abbey says:** These would be adorable as place cards: just pipe each guest's name on his or her sled.
- **Margie says:** For festive presentation, place your favorite Christmas novelties atop the sleds.

Winter Boots

A perfect pair of winter boots to keep you stylish and warm.
These cookies look like they would be lined with fur.

✳ ✳ ❄ ✳ ✳

WHAT YOU NEED:

Parchment paper
Fondant rolling pin
Brown fondant
Boot cookie cutter
Offset spatula
2 Paintbrushes
Corn syrup
Boot cookies
Black fondant
Gold Pearl Luster Dust
Fork
Pastry bag with #2 tip
Black royal icing
White royal icing
Bow
Dragées

DIRECTIONS:

Roll brown fondant on parchment paper to ⅛-inch thickness. Cut into boot shapes with your boot cookie cutter.

Using an offset spatula, cut the bottom part of each boot away from the top of the boot, in a stylish fashion. Discard the top of boot. Set the fondant boots aside.

With a paintbrush, dab corn syrup on the top of each cookie. Carefully place the fondant on top of the syrup, smoothing the edges with a dry finger.

Repeat the above steps with black fondant, this time reserving the tops and discarding the bottoms of the boots.

Use a dry paintbrush to dust the fondant with luster dust.

With the tines of a fork, create linear detail patterns on the boot, to look like stitching.

With black royal icing in your pastry bag, pipe the sole detail of each boot.

Using a new pastry bag filled with white royal icing, pipe detail for the top of each boot.

Use additional icing to adhere the bow and the dragées to each boot.

Let dry for at least one hour or until the royal icing is hardened.

Tip: Sometimes when creating a stitching pattern with fork tines, the dots do not always line up perfectly straight on the fondant. A new dressmaker's wheel (or a new hair comb) works great for making straight, long lines.

Cup of Hot Cocoa

Margie says: I love black and white. This is what a cup of hot chocolate looks like at my house.

✳ ✳ ❄ ✳ ✳

WHAT YOU NEED:

Parchment paper

Pastry bag with #2 tip

White royal icing

Fondant rolling pin

Black fondant

White fondant

Teacup-and-Saucer cookie cutter

Offset spatula

4 Paintbrushes

Corn syrup

Teacup cookie

Mini Teardrop cookie cutter

Brown fondant

Super Pearl Luster Dust

Mini marshmallows

DIRECTIONS:

Using your pastry bag, pipe quarter-sized dollops of white royal icing onto the parchment paper in a circular motion to look like whipped cream. Let the icing dry on the parchment until hard (a few hours or overnight). The "whipped cream" can be made a day or so ahead of time.

Roll the black fondant on parchment paper to $1/8$-inch thickness. Using white fondant, make pea-sized balls and place them on the rolled black fondant. Roll the fondant out again until the white fondant is incorporated into the black.

Use a teacup-and-saucer cookie cutter to cut the fondant. With an offset spatula, separate the saucers from the cups. Discard the cups. Dab corn syrup on top of each cookie, where the saucer will rest. Place a fondant saucer on each cookie, smoothing the edges with a dry finger.

Roll white fondant on parchment paper to $1/8$-inch thickness. This time using black fondant, again make pea-sized balls and place them on the rolled fondant. Roll the fondant out again until the black fondant is incorporated into the white.

Use your teacup cookie cutter to cut the fondant. Cut the area for the brown fondant from the cups and discard along with the saucers. Use your teardrop cutter to cut the handle of each cup. Dab corn syrup on each cookie where the fondant teacup will rest. Place a fondant cup on each cookie, smoothing the edges with a dry finger.

Roll the brown fondant on parchment paper to $1/8$-inch thickness. Use the cookie cutter again to cut pieces that look like hot chocolate. Dab corn syrup on top of each cookie, where the "cocoa" will rest. Place the fondant on the syrup layer, smoothing the edges with your finger.

Use a dry paintbrush to brush the entire cookie with luster dust.

With white royal icing in your pastry bag, and a #2 tip, pipe the detail of the seam of each cup and saucer. Use additional icing to adhere the marshmallows to the saucers and the dollops of "whipped cream" to the tops.

Let dry for at least one hour or until the icing is hardened.

Polar Bears

Margie says: I have always wanted to travel to the Arctic region to see the solitary, majestic polar bear perched on the ice as it floats along the coastline.

✳ ✳ ❄ ✳ ✳

WHAT YOU NEED:

6-inch ribbons (⅛-inch wide,
one for each cookie),
plus extra ribbon for bows
Parchment paper
Fondant rolling pin
White fondant
Striped textured rolling pin
Polar bear cookie cutter
Paintbrush
Corn syrup
Polar bear cookie
White royal icing
Candy stars
Pastry bag with #2 tip
White sanding sugar
Black royal icing

DIRECTIONS:

Using the extra ribbon, make enough small bows for each cookie. Set aside.

Roll the fondant on parchment paper to ⅛-inch thickness.

Using a striped textured rolling pin, roll over the fondant one time. Cut it into polar bear shapes with your cookie cutter. Set aside.

With a paintbrush, dab corn syrup on top of each cookie. Carefully place a fondant bear on top of the syrup, smoothing the edges with a dry finger.

To add the necklaces, carefully place the middle of a ribbon on each bear's neck, and wrap the ribbon around the neck on both the front and back sides of the cookie. Allow the remainder to hang below the neck. Secure the cut edges of the ribbon together with white royal icing.

Use additional icing to adhere a candy star to the bottom of each ribbon, to join the two ribbon edges together, and to secure a small bow to the top of each necklace.

With white royal icing in your pastry bag, pipe an outline of the body of your bear.

Sprinkle sanding sugar on the icing. Flip each cookie once to remove excess sugar.

With black royal icing in your pastry bag, pipe the eye, nose, and foot detail of each bear.

Let dry for at least one hour or until the royal icing is hardened.

• **Margie says:** I used a textured rolling pin to give the look of fur.

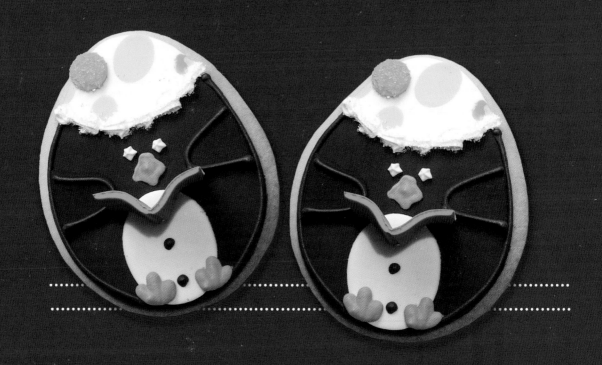

✳✳✳✳✳

FESTIVITIES

✳✳✳✳✳

Mummer's Banjos

Mention New Year's Day in Philadelphia and immediately, images of the Mummers Parade, with its many string bands, come to mind.

✳ ✳ ✾ ✳ ✳

We used the star cookie cutter as a "manufacturer's label."
Personalize your banjo with any small cutter as your own label.

WHAT YOU NEED:

Parchment paper
Fondant rolling pin
White fondant
Banjo cookie cutter
Utility knife
Offset spatula
Paintbrush
Corn syrup
Banjo cookies
Mini star cookie cutter
(optional)
Black fondant
Scissors
Thin ribbon (⅛-inch)
Black royal icing
Pastry bag with #2 tip
Gold dragées
Jujubes, licorice, and PEZ or
similar assorted candies

DIRECTIONS:

Roll the white fondant on parchment paper to ⅛-inch thickness.

Using your banjo cookie cutter, cut enough fondant banjos for your batch of cookies. Cut the neck from each fondant banjo. Use the paintbrush to dab corn syrup on the banjo body of each cookie. Place the fondant body on top of the syrup, smoothing the edges with your finger. Use the mini star cutter to gently press an indentation into the fondant, if desired.

Roll the black fondant on parchment paper to ⅛-inch thickness.

Using the banjo cookie cutter, cut enough fondant banjos for your batch of cookies. Cut off the bodies of the fondant banjo. Dab corn syrup on just the necks of each cookie. Place the fondant neck on the syrup, smoothing the edges with your finger.

Cut two ribbon pieces for each cookie.

Pipe black royal icing around the outer edge of each banjo body. Adhere gold dragées to the icing. Stretch the reserved ribbons down the length of the cookie, to make the banjo strings. Make sure the ends are attached securely to the icing.

To decorate: Use additional icing to adhere the candies to each banjo. PEZ candies work well for the bridge. Jujubes make great tuners. Use black icing to pipe the tuner details. Let the cookies dry for at least one hour.

Note: The PEZ candies help secure the ribbons to the cookies, so they won't wiggle around.

Feliz Navidad

Growing up in the Northeast, Christmas meant evergreens and cold weather.
In Mexico, it's mild weather and palm trees decked out in Christmas lights!

WHAT YOU NEED:

Parchment paper
Fondant rolling pin
Red fondant
Mini Star cookie cutter
2 Paintbrushes
Gold Pearl Luster Dust
Green fondant
Palm tree cookie cutter
Offset spatula
Corn syrup
Palm tree cookies
Brown fondant
Textured fondant rolling pin
Pastry bags with #2 tip
Leaf green royal icing
Electric green royal icing
M&M's or similar candies (2 per
cookie, to hold the stars
upright)
White fondant
Black royal icing
Assorted royal icing colors
for lights

DIRECTIONS:

To make the stars, roll red fondant on parchment paper to ⅛-inch thickness. Cut mini stars (two per cookie) with your star cookie cutter. Dust the fondant star with luster dust. Set aside until hard. These can be made a day or so ahead of time.

To make the tree, roll green fondant on parchment paper to ⅛-inch thickness. Cut it into tree shapes with your tree cookie cutter. Cut the trunk from the fronds. Dab corn syrup on top of each cookie, where the fronds will rest. Place the fronds on the syrup layer, smoothing the edges with your finger. Dust the fronds with luster dust.

Roll the brown fondant on parchment paper to ⅛-inch thickness. Roll over the fondant once more with a textured rolling pin. Cut palm trees with your tree cutter. Cut the fronds from the trunk. Dab corn syrup on top of each cookie's trunk. Place the fondant trunks on the syrup layer, smoothing the edges with your finger. Dust each trunk with luster dust.

Pipe the frond detail with the leaf green royal icing.

Pipe additional detail using the electric green icing.

Adhere the reserved fondant stars to the icing, two per cookie, on the palm fronds.

Use candies to prop each star upright.

For the trunk, use black royal icing to pipe the string detail. Finish with royal icing dots in assorted colors. Let dry for at least one hour or until the icing is hardened.

Penguin Parade of Carolers

Margie says: Imagine looking out the window and seeing this parade of penguins wobbling down the street, singing Christmas carols! These penguins are so plump—the image makes me chuckle!

* * ❇ * *

Toothpicks are great tools for removing sanding sugar from places you do not want it.

WHAT YOU NEED:

Parchment paper
Fondant rolling pin
Accent colors of fondant (red, blue, green, purple)
Mini Rectangle cookie cutter (for songbooks)
Toothpick
Black fondant
Egg (or oval) cookie cutter
Paintbrush
Corn syrup
Oval cookie
Black royal icing
Pastry bag with #1 tip
White fondant
Mini oval cookie cutter
Pastry bag with star tip
Pastry bag with #2 tip

DIRECTIONS:

To make the 3-D songbook, roll accent colors of fondant on parchment paper to $\frac{1}{8}$-inch thickness. Cut into rectangles with your rectangle cookie cutter.

Using a toothpick, score the middle of each rectangle to look like the center of an open book. Bend each book in half and create shape by propping the two sides on the lip of a cookie tray. Let dry for at least one hour or until hardened. These can be made a day or so ahead of time.

To make the penguins, roll black fondant on parchment paper to $\frac{1}{8}$-inch thickness. Cut into ovals with your egg cookie cutter.

Use the edge of the cutter to cut away the top of each oval, to create a shape for the penguin's cap.

With a paintbrush, dab corn syrup on top of each cookie. Carefully place the fondant on the syrup layer, smoothing the edges with a dry finger. Set aside.

You can make raised arms by rolling out black fondant, cutting out half ovals, adhering them to the sides of the body with corn syrup, and then piping black icing from the pastry bag with a #1 tip to outline them. Or you can just pipe the black icing into a half oval at the edges of the penguin body. Set aside.

Roll white fondant on parchment paper to $\frac{1}{8}$-inch thickness. Cut into ovals with your oval mini cookie cutter. Attach an oval to the belly of each penguin, with royal icing.

White royal icing
Sanding sugar
Orange royal icing

Roll additional white fondant to $1/8$-inch thickness. Set aside.

With your hands, use your accent colors of fondant to create thin ropes (for stripes) and balls (for dots). Lay these on the white fondant, and roll with the fondant pin until the colors are completely integrated into one smooth surface. Cut the fondant with your egg cookie cutter. Use the edge of the cutter to cut away the top of the egg to create the penguin's cap.

To decorate: Working with one cookie at a time, use a star tip and white royal icing in your pastry bag to cover the seam of the cap and make the eyes.

Sprinkle white sanding sugar on the icing, and tip the cookie over once to shake off the excess.

With black royal icing, in a pastry bag with a #1 tip, outline the body and pipe the arm detail and the dots on the belly.

With orange royal icing, in a pastry bag with a # 2 tip, pipe the nose and the feet.

Use white royal icing and a star tip to create two starry eyes. Use additional white royal icing to adhere the premade songbooks and gumdrops.

Let dry for at least one hour or until the icing is hardened.

Tip: It is important to pipe the detail with sanding sugar before the detail without sanding sugar. Otherwise everything will have sanding sugar on it (which may be nice too)! And don't worry if the cap and the penguin body do not align perfectly. You will cover the seam with royal icing.

New Year's Eve Shoes

Margie says: Every New Year's Eve my husband and I go to our dear friends the Rosens' house. Louis and Leslie are fabulous caterers in Philadelphia. For the thirty-five years we have been going, year after year it has been the most elegant and festive dinner party I attend. We get dressed up for the occasion, and I think these shoes would be perfect.

✳ ✳ ❇ ✳ ✳

If you do not have time to create fondant roses, any premade
sugar flower will work, as long as the base is flat. When making roses
it's OK if the petals tear a bit, because it creates the effect of a natural rose.

WHAT YOU NEED:

Black fondant (for roses)
Ball tool (for petals)
Offset spatula
Parchment paper
Fondant rolling pin
Red fondant
Shoe cookie cutter
2 Paintbrushes
Corn syrup
Shoe cookies
White fondant
Edible metallic paint
Vodka or lemon extract
Pastry bag with #2 tip
Red royal icing

DIRECTIONS:

To make the fondant roses, shape small pieces of black fondant into small ($\frac{1}{8}$-inch) cone shapes to make the buds. Set the buds aside.

For the petals, start by using the black fondant to create little ($\frac{1}{4}$-inch) balls, one for each flower. With your thumb, push the center of each ball to create a flat petal. (Press your thumb in a small amount of cornstarch before you flatten the ball, so the fondant doesn't stick to your finger.)

With the petal on the foam pad, use the ball tool in a circular motion to soften the edges and create a slight bowl shape. Wrap the petals around the cone-shaped bud and press together at the bottom so it becomes one piece. The fondant will adhere to itself with a dab of water. Only create a few petals at a time, or else they will dry out and not adhere well to the bud. Attach as many petals as you would like, by overlapping them; then pull the top of the petals away from the bud to open the rose. The more petals you add, the larger the flower will be.

Use an offset spatula to slice the bottom stem and create a flat base.

Allow the flowers to set by standing them upright against the edge of a pan or by

Red ribbon (for bows)
Foam pad (for using ball tool
on petals)
Super Pearl Luster Dust

inserting a toothpick into them and standing them in a Styrofoam base to harden.

To make the shoes, roll red fondant on parchment paper to $\frac{1}{8}$-inch thickness. Cut it into shoe shapes with your shoe cookie cutter. At an angle, use the offset spatula to cut off the heel (the heel will be replaced by a separate piece of fondant). Discard the heels. Set the fondant shoes aside.

With a paintbrush, dab corn syrup on top of each cookie. Carefully place the reserved fondant shoes on the syrup layer, smoothing the edges with a dry finger. Set prepared cookies aside.

Roll the white fondant on parchment paper to $\frac{1}{8}$-inch thickness. Again, use the cookie cutter to cut the fondant into shoes, and the spatula to cut off the heels. This time, reserve the heels, and discard the rest of the shoe.

Carefully place the heels on the cookies, smoothing the edges with a dry finger. Add a little more corn syrup if the heels don't stick.

In a small container, combine a dash of the edible paint with a touch of vodka. Stir to create a paste. Paint three coats of paste over the white fondant heels, letting the paste dry between coats.

Using the same paste, paint the edges of the petals of each flower. Make some bows out of your red ribbon. Using a pastry bag filled with red royal icing, pipe the outline of each shoe. Use additional icing to adhere the roses and bows.

Let the cookies dry for at least one hour or until the icing is hardened.

Tip: Be careful to clean off the cutter after you use the red fondant. You do not want red residue showing on the white fondant.

- **Abbey says:** This is a fast version of the roses you may see on a cake. But because the cookie is small, the rose should be proportional, so it doesn't have to be as intricate. As Margie says, "Don't get crazy!"
- **Margie says:** Any dark-color fondant requires a lot of dye—for example, red and black. You may need more cornstarch than normal, because darker colors can be stickier than lighter ones.

Twinkle, Twinkle, Gold Stars

To give these shortbread cookie cutouts a festive holiday touch,
we added fondant and painted them gold!

WHAT YOU NEED:

Parchment paper

Fondant rolling pin

White fondant

Star cookie cutter

White royal icing

Pastry bag with #2 tip

Star cookies (see Chocolate
Chip Shortbread
Cookie Dough recipe,
page 129)

Edible gold powder

Drop of vodka or lemon
extract

Paintbrush

Small bowl

Dragées

DIRECTIONS:

Roll white fondant on parchment paper to $\frac{1}{8}$-inch thickness. Cut it into star shapes with your star cookie cutter. Set aside.

With white royal icing in your pastry bag, pipe the tops of your cookies with enough icing to secure the fondant stars. Ice only those areas where the fondant stars will rest.

Carefully place the fondant stars on the cookies, smoothing the edges with a dry finger. Then pipe around the outer edges of each star. Let dry for at least one hour.

In a small bowl, mix the gold powder with a drop of vodka to make a paste. (If the paste becomes too thin, add more powder.)

With a dry paintbrush, paint the fondant with the edible gold paint. (You may need several coats; let dry between coats.) Pipe a dot in the center of each star to adhere a dragée.

Let the cookies dry for at least one hour or until the icing is hardened.

* * * * *

HOME FOR
THE HOLIDAYS

* * * * *

Gingerbread Houses

*Abbey says: For several years, our bakery was in an old Victorian house.
Every Christmas we would decorate the house with garland and lights.
When it snowed, the icicles would drip from the house trim. It was beautiful.*

❋ ❋ ❋ ❋ ❋

This is an excellent exercise in piping straight lines.
We recommend practicing lines on parchment paper before working on your cookie.

WHAT YOU NEED:

White royal icing
Pastry bag with #2 tip
Gingerbread House cookies
(see Gingerbread Cookie
Dough recipe, page 127)
Pastry bag with #4 tip
White sanding sugar
Parchment paper
Green royal icing
Red royal icing
Yellow royal icing

DIRECTIONS:

With white royal icing in your pastry bag, and a #2 tip, pipe the framework detail (windows, doors, etc.) on your gingerbread houses.

Use white royal icing in a pastry bag with a #4 tip to create the appearance of a snow-topped roof. Sprinkle sanding sugar where desired, to look like snow. Let dry.

Using the pastry bag with the #2 tip, pipe the finishing details.

Use green royal icing for the garland.

Use red icing for the candles, windows, and door.

Use yellow icing for the candles' flames.

- **Margie says:** It's fun to fashion many houses with different facades to create a village lined on your mantelpiece.

51

Wreath

Margie says: This is a great project to do ahead, and to do with kids. Simply make the leaves in advance, and assemble at your leisure.

✳ ✳ ❋ ✳ ✳

Pearl luster dust really gives the leaves added dimension because it highlights the veins. Make sure to apply the pearl dust while the fondant is still soft.

WHAT YOU NEED:

Parchment paper
Fondant rolling pin
Green fondant (enough for leaves and for wreath)
Leaf cookie cutter
Toothpick
White fondant
Super Pearl Luster Dust
Super Red Luster Dust
Lime Green Luster Dust
Wreath cookie cutter (or a 6-inch and a 4-inch circle cutter)
2 Paintbrushes
Corn syrup
Wreath cookie
Green royal icing
Pastry bag with #2 tip
Dragées
Bow

DIRECTIONS:

To make the leaves, roll green fondant on parchment paper to $1/8$-inch thickness. Cut 30 to 35 leaves with your leaf cookie cutter. Use a toothpick to create veins. Brush the leaves with pearl luster dust. Prop the leaves on the lip of a baking sheet to curl the edges when drying. Let harden, about one hour.

To make the ornaments, roll white fondant into $1/4$- to $1/2$-inch balls in your palm. Put $1/8$ teaspoon of red luster dust in your palm and roll half of the fondant balls until coated. Repeat with the lime green luster dust for the remaining balls.

Roll green fondant on parchment paper to $1/8$-inch thickness. Cut it into wreath shape with your wreath cookie cutter. With a paintbrush, dab corn syrup on top of each wreath cookie. Place the fondant wreath on the syrup layer, smoothing the edges with a dry finger.

Beginning at the top of each wreath, lay the fondant leaves in an overlapping pattern, working randomly around the wreath. Use royal icing in a pastry bag to adhere the leaves to the cookie.

To decorate: Use additional royal icing to adhere the ornaments and dragées to the leaves. Finish with a decorative bow. Let dry for at least one hour or until the icing is dry.

Fireplace

✳ ✳ ✳ ✳ ✳

We used Necco wafers to look like stones on the fireplace.
You can also try using Pez candies to give the appearance of brick.

WHAT YOU NEED:

Lollipop stick

Parchment paper

Fondant rolling pin

Red or green fondant

Mini stocking cutter

2 Pastry bags with #2 tips

Red or lime green royal icing

White royal icing

Chocolate fondant

Rectangle cookie cutter

3 Paintbrushes

Corn syrup

1 rectangle cookie for fireplace

2 half-rectangle cookies for mantel and base

Black fondant

Square cookie cutter

Yellow fondant

Orange fondant

Fire template, (page 136)

DIRECTIONS:

To make the stockings, roll red or green fondant on parchment paper to $\frac{1}{8}$-inch thickness. Cut the fondant with your stocking cutter.

Using a #2 tip on your pastry bag, and either red or lime green royal icing, pipe the bottom detail of each stocking. Use white royal icing in the other pastry bag with a #2 tip to pipe the top of each stocking. Adhere a bow to the top right corner of the white royal icing. Set aside and let dry for at least one hour or until the fondant and icing are hardened.

To make the mantel, roll chocolate fondant on parchment paper to $\frac{1}{8}$-inch thickness.

Cut the fondant into a rectangle with your large rectangule cookie cutter and cut that in half lengthwise. With a paintbrush, dab corn syrup on top of each half-rectangle cookie. Carefully place the precut fondant half rectangles on top of each cookie, smoothing the edges with a dry finger. Set aside.

To make the fireplace body, roll black fondant on parchment paper to $\frac{1}{8}$-inch thickness. Cut into a square with a square cookie cutter. With a paintbrush, dab corn syrup on top of the large rectangle cookie, where the opening of the fireplace will go. Carefully place the fondant square on the cookie, smoothing the edges with a dry finger.

With your hands, swirl together the yellow and orange fondant. Roll the swirled fondant on parchment paper to $\frac{1}{8}$-inch thickness. Place the fire template on the

Utility knife
Offset spatula
Super Pearl Luster Dust
Brown royal icing
Necco wafers
2 half-rectangle cookies, one
for the mantel and one
for the base
Green royal icing
Pastry bag with #233 tip
Dragées
Yellow royal icing
Tootsie Rolls
Pastry bag with #18 star tip

fondant and cut out the fire with the utility knife. Remove the fire with an offset spatula. Place a dab of corn syrup with a paintbrush on the black square fondant; then place the fondant fire on the black square. Smooth the edges with a dry finger.

Use a dry paintbrush to dust the fire with luster dust.

Use a clean paintbrush to spread brown royal icing on the exposed area of the cookie. Place broken bits of Necco wafers to give the appearance of stone. Work in small batches so the icing does not dry.

With brown royal icing in your pastry bag, and a #2 tip, pipe detail around the opening of the fireplace. Let dry for at least one hour or until the icing is hardened.

While that's drying decorate the mantel. With green royal icing in your pastry bag, and a #233 tip, pipe pine greens on top of the mantel (one of the brown fondanted half rectangles). While the icing is wet, adhere the dragées and cut lollipop sticks to create the pillar candles.

With yellow royal icing in your pastry bag, and a #2 tip, pipe the flame detail on top of the candles. Let dry for at least one hour or until you can easily work with the mantel without smudging the icing. Set mantel aside.

When the fireplace is dry, attach the base (the remaining brown fondanted half rectangle) to the fireplace by piping additional brown icing along the bottom of the cookie. Adhere the base to the body. Prop up with either a mug or another sturdy item so the icing can dry. Let dry for at least one hour or until hardened. In the same fashion, attach the mantel to the body.

Use royal icing in a pastry bag with a #2 tip and adhere the stockings to the mantel. Let dry for at least one hour or until hardened.

Use royal icing to adhere the Tootsie Rolls to the base of each fireplace, stacked to look like logs.

Tip: If you don't have a lollipop stick to create pillar candles, Good & Plenty candies, or even thin pretzel sticks work well.

Reindeer Stockings

What I was doing, sawing away and trying to cut pretzel sticks on an angle,
was a mystery to Richard, our head baker—until, voilà! An antler appeared.
A bit tedious—not to mention the collection of pretzels thrown all over the table
by the end of the task—but I think the effect is worth it.

✳ ✳ ❄ ✳ ✳

WHAT YOU NEED:

Thin pretzel sticks
Serrated knife
Brown royal icing
Pastry bags with #2 tip
Assorted colors of royal icing
for lights and antler detail
Parchment paper
Fondant rolling pin
Chocolate fondant
Stocking cookie cutter
Offset spatula
Paintbrush
Corn syrup
Stocking cookies
Scissors
Ribbon
White fondant

DIRECTIONS:

To make the antlers, set aside one thin pretzel stick as the center of each antler. Use a knife to cut the other pretzel pieces at an angle.

Attach these angled pieces to the main antler, with brown royal icing. (Don't worry if the icing shows on the antler.) Lay the antlers flat to let the icing dry.

When dry, use a pastry bag with assorted colors to pipe dots on the antlers, to resemble Christmas lights. Let dry.

To make the stockings, roll chocolate fondant on parchment paper to $\frac{1}{8}$-inch thickness. Cut it with your stocking cookie cutter.

Using an offset spatula, cut the cuff from each stocking body. Discard the cuffs. Set the stockings aside.

With a paintbrush, dab corn syrup on top of each cookie. Carefully place the fondant stocking pieces on the syrup layer, smoothing the edges with a dry finger.

Use scissors to cut a piece of red ribbon for each cookie. Create a loop, and use royal icing to adhere a ribbon to the top of each cookie, at the cuff.

Roll white fondant on parchment paper to $\frac{1}{8}$-inch thickness. Set aside.

Tip: Want less mess? Pipe the antlers in with brown royal icing, flat onto the cookie. It looks cute either way.

Red fondant
White royal icing
White sanding sugar
Red royal icing
Black royal icing
Brown royal icing
Pastry bag with leaf tip
Red M&M's or similar candies
Bows (one per cookie)

With your hands, shape red fondant into pea-sized balls. Place the balls on the white fondant and roll over both with a rolling pin until incorporated into one piece.

Cut with your stocking cookie cutter; then use the spatula to cut the cuff from each stocking body. This time, discard the stocking bodies.

With a paintbrush, dab corn syrup on top of each cookie. Carefully place the fondant cuffs on the syrup layer, smoothing the edges with a dry finger. (Don't worry if the cuff and stocking body do not meet; you will cover the seam with royal icing.)

To decorate: Use white royal icing to pipe the cuff and eye detail, and to cover the seam between the cuff and stocking body. Sprinkle white sanding sugar on top of the seam, for sparkle. Use red royal icing to make red dots on the cuff for texture.

Use black royal icing to finish the eye. Use brown royal icing in a pastry bag with a leaf tip to pipe an ear. Use additional royal icing to affix a red candy at the toe of each stocking, for the nose, and to adhere the antlers. Use a nickel-sized piece of wadded paper towel ball to hold the antlers in place while drying. Finally, add a bow to the base of the antler, to hide the juncture of the antler to the stocking. Let dry.

Tip: Make sure the brown icing is very stiff so the ear will hold its shape.

String of Lights

In his family, our head baker, Richard, was in charge of checking each and
every bulb on his strings of Christmas lights. He claims that he never, ever got his
lights tangled together. It makes sense: you should see how organized he is in the kitchen!
We dedicate these lights to Richard.

✳ ✳ ❄ ✳ ✳

These are also fun in just red and green.
For presentation, lay a piece of licorice on the platter, as the string.

WHAT YOU NEED:

Parchment paper
Fondant rolling pin
Colored fondant
Light cookie cutter
2 Paintbrushes
Corn syrup
Christmas light cookie
Toothpick
Gold edible paint
Vodka or lemon extract

DIRECTIONS:

Roll colored fondant on parchment paper to $\frac{1}{8}$-inch thickness. Cut each rolled sheet with your light cookie cutter. Set aside.

With a paintbrush, dab corn syrup on top of each cookie. Carefully place the fondant light on top of the syrup layer, smoothing the edges with a dry finger. Repeat with different colors.

Create ridges on the base of each light bulb by pressing a toothpick into the fondant horizontally. Set cookies aside.

In a small bowl, mix a dash of gold edible paint with a few drops of liquid (vodka or lemon extract) to make a paste.

Use a dry paintbrush to paint the top of each light bulb. Depending on how much coverage you want, let the paste dry between coats, and repeat as necessary.

Let the cookies dry for at least one hour or until the fondant is hardened.

✳

FESTIVAL OF LIGHTS

✳

Stacks of Presents

Abbey says: Before Hanukah, my mom would stay up late at night to wrap Hanukah presents. Be it a bag of gelt or a fun little novelty, opening my mom's wrapped presents was and is like opening two presents in one.

✳ ✳ ❇ ✳ ✳

This stacked present cookie is really a tiered-cake cookie cutter shape!

WHAT YOU NEED:

Parchment paper
Fondant rolling pin
White fondant
Blue fondant
Tiered-cake cookie cutter
Offset spatula
2 paintbrushes
Corn syrup
Cake cookie
Yellow fondant
Purple fondant
Additional white fondant
Edible metallic paint
Vodka
Pastry bag with #2 tip
Blue royal icing
White royal icing
Bows
Dragées
Candy confetti

DIRECTIONS:

For the top tier, roll white fondant on parchment paper to $1/8$-inch thickness. Use the cookie cutter to cut fondant. Separate top tier with edge of cutter. Dab corn syrup on the surface of the top of the cookie. Adhere fondant and smooth edges.

For the third tier, repeat using blue fondant.

For the second tier, roll white fondant on parchment paper to $1/8$-inch thickness. Shape blue fondant into pea-sized balls and place them on the rolled fondant. Roll the fondant out again until the balls are incorporated into the fondant. Cut fondant and adhere fondant as before but for the second tier.

For the first or bottom tier, repeat the process with blue fondant. Make yellow fondant stripes instead of polka dots.

Mix a dash of edible metallic paint with a touch of vodka to create a paste. Using a dry paintbrush, paint the white fondant tier with the paste. Let dry. Repeat three times, letting each coat dry before applying the next.

Using a pastry bag with a #2 tip, pipe the present outline with white royal icing. Use blue royal icing to add present detail. Adhere the bows, dragées, and candy confetti with royal icing. Let dry for at least one hour or until the royal icing is hardened.

Chocolate Stars of David

The sweetness of these chocolate cookies pairs perfectly with the saltiness of potato latkes. After experimenting with different cocoas for our chocolate recipe, we feel that this is our best chocolate cookie recipe yet.

WHAT YOU NEED:

Colored royal icing

Pastry bag with #2 tip

Menorah sugar shapes

Star cookies (see Chocolate Cookie Dough recipe, page 128)

DIRECTIONS:

With royal icing in your pastry bag, pipe star detail around the edges of the star cookies.

Adhere sugar shapes to the center of each cookie using royal icing.

Tip: Sugar shapes come in all shapes and sizes. We like the menorahs as well as stars and dreidels.

• **Abbey says:** My nieces Hallie and Sara love cookie decorating. This is a perfect cookie for kids to lend a helping hand. I dab a bit of royal icing on each cookie, and put the girls in charge of placing the sugar shapes on top.

• **Margie says:** I like the darkness of this chocolate cookie. Some chocolate recipes are too light in color. This one looks like it tastes: fudgy and rich.

Dreidel, Dreidel, Dreidel

Margie says: *Every year for Hanukah, I give each of my three children the same decorative dreidel. We always open them together on the same day, and it's my favorite Hanukah tradition.*

WHAT YOU NEED:

Kite cookie cutter
(for Dreidel cookies)
Utility knife
Parchment paper
Fondant rolling pin
Purple fondant
Offset spatula
Paintbrush
Corn syrup
Dreidel cookies
Turquoise fondant
Blue fondant
White royal icing
Pastry bag with #2 tip
Candied licorice or similar
candy, for spinners

DIRECTIONS:

To make the right side of the dreidel, roll purple fondant on parchment paper to $\frac{1}{8}$-inch thickness. Cut it into dreidel shapes with your cookie cutter. Using a utility knife, cut out the right triangle. (It is important for the outside edges to be the neatest.) Dab corn syrup on top of each cookie, where the right fondant piece will rest. Place the fondant on the syrup, smoothing the edges with a dry finger.

To make the left side of the dreidel, roll turquoise fondant on parchment paper to $\frac{1}{8}$-inch thickness. Cut it with your cookie cutter. Cut out the left triangle. Dab corn syrup on top of each cookie, where the left fondant piece will rest. Place the fondant on the syrup, again smoothing the edges with a dry finger. (The edges that will touch will be covered by piping, so it's okay if the fondant doesn't align perfectly.)

To make the top, roll blue fondant on parchment paper to $\frac{1}{8}$-inch thickness. Cut out the top triangle. Dab corn syrup on top of each cookie, where the top fondant piece will rest. Place the fondant on the syrup, smoothing the edges with a dry finger.

With white royal icing in your pastry bag, pipe around the edges and down the center of each of the three colors of fondant and pipe the Hebrew letters.

Add a spinner of candy licorice (or Good & Plenty or Mike and Ike) using icing. Let dry for at least one hour or until the icing is hardened.

Tip: To create turquoise fondant, combine leaf green, sky blue, and warm brown gel paste. For a simpler design, use a single color of fondant.

*****

PEPPERMINT STRIPES

*****

Candy Ornaments

We use buckets and buckets of peppermint candies at The Flour Pot during Christmas. They become pom-poms, wheels, and other whimsical adornments on many of our cookies.

✳ ✳ ❄ ✳ ✳

WHAT YOU NEED:

Parchment paper

Fondant rolling pin

White fondant

Circle cookie cutter

2 Paintbrushes

Corn syrup

Circle cookies

Red and/or green fondant

Utility knife

Swirl template (page 136)

Fork

Super Pearl Luster Dust

White royal icing

Pastry bag with #2 tip

Peppermint candies or green and white mints

Ribbon for hanging cookies, and ribbon bows

DIRECTIONS:

Roll white fondant on parchment paper to $\frac{1}{8}$-inch thickness. Cut it into circles with your circle cookie cutter. Set aside.

With a paintbrush, dab corn syrup on top of each cookie. Carefully place the fondant on the syrup layer, smoothing the edges with a dry finger. Set aside.

Roll red or green fondant on parchment paper to $\frac{1}{8}$-inch thickness. Using a utility knife and your swirl template, carefully cut five swirls for each cookie.

Adhere the swirl pieces to the white fondant circles with a dab of royal icing, in a pinwheel pattern. (Do not worry if the stripes do not meet in the center; it will be covered with a peppermint.) Smooth edges with your fingers.

Create edging detail of the swirl with the tines of a fork. The edges here are the most important part. You want the outside edges of the peppermint swirls to be completely blended into the white.

Use a dry paintbrush to dust the entire cookie with luster dust to add a shimmer.

Use royal icing to adhere a peppermint candy to the center of each cookie, on top of the swirls.

With ribbon, create a loop for each cookie, and adhere the loop and a bow to the top of the cookie with royal icing.

Let dry for at least one hour or until the icing is hardened.

Tip: Be sure to cut the template pieces all the same way. Mark the template with a T *for* top *as a reminder.*

Peppermint on the Rocks

What better way to celebrate the holidays than with a festive Christmas cocktail.

❄ ❄ ❄ ❄ ❄

WHAT YOU NEED:

Scissors

Ribbon

Toothpick

Peppermint candy

Parchment paper

Fondant rolling pin

Green fondant

Martini or parfait glass–
shaped cookie cutter

Offset spatula

2 Paintbrushes

Corn syrup

Martini or parfait
glass cookies

Super Pearl Luster Dust

Red fondant

Green royal icing

Pastry bags with #2 tip

Red royal icing

DIRECTIONS:

To make the stirrers, cut enough ribbons for all of your cookies. Tie each ribbon around a toothpick. Attach a peppermint candy to each toothpick with white royal icing. Let dry.

To make the glasses, roll green fondant on parchment paper to $1/8$-inch thickness. Cut it with your glass cookie cutter. Use an offset spatula to cut the base from each glass. Discard the bases. Set the glasses aside.

With a paintbrush, dab corn syrup on top of each cookie, where the bowl of each glass will rest. Carefully place the green fondant pieces on the syrup layer, smoothing the edges with a dry finger. Use a dry paintbrush to dust with luster dust.

Roll the red fondant on parchment paper to $1/8$-inch thickness. Cut it with your glass cookie cutter. Use the spatula to cut the base from each glass, this time discarding the glass. Set the bases aside.

With a paintbrush, dab corn syrup on the bottom of each cookie, where the base of each glass will rest. Carefully place the fondant bases on the syrup layer, smoothing the edges with a dry finger. Dust with luster dust.

With green royal icing in your pastry bag, pipe the outline of each glass. Attach a peppermint stirrer to the royal icing.

Using a new pastry bag filled with red royal icing, pipe dots on the glass bases.

Let dry for at least one hour or until the icing is hardened.

Tip: We use sandwich toothpicks rather than regular toothpicks. They are long and wide, and they lie flat.

Ho Ho Ho

What makes these cookies whimsical is the off-center O.
We love the unexpected hint of Santa.

✳ ✳ ❇ ✳ ✳

WHAT YOU NEED:

Parchment paper

Fondant rolling pin

Red fondant (for Santa hats
and for stripes)

Santa hat template
(page 136)

Utility knife

White fondant

Green fondant

H cookie cutter

O cookie cutter

2 Paintbrushes

Corn syrup

H- and O-shaped cookies

Super Pearl Luster Dust

White royal icing

Pastry bag with star tip

Sanding sugar

DIRECTIONS:

Roll red fondant on parchment paper to $\frac{1}{8}$-inch thickness. Place the Santa hat template on the fondant and cut out the hat with the utility knife. Using an offset spatula, remove the hat and set aside. Let dry for at least one hour or until hardened.

Roll white fondant on parchment paper to $\frac{1}{8}$-inch thickness.

With your hands, create thin ropes of green and red fondant. Lay the ropes on top of the white rolled fondant.

Roll with the fondant pin until the ropes are integrated into the white fondant in one smooth surface.

Cut the fondant into H's and O's with your letter cookie cutters. Set the fondant letters aside.

With a paintbrush, dab corn syrup on top of each cookie. Carefully place the fondant letters on the cookies, smoothing the edges with a dry finger. Use a dry paintbrush to dust with luster dust. Repeat for each letter.

Attach the red hats to the O fondant letters with white royal icing.

With the pastry bag with the star tip and white icing, pipe the detail and pom-poms.

Sprinkle white sanding sugar on the icing. Flip cookies over once to shake off the excess sugar.

Let dry for at least one hour or until the icing is hardened.

Tip: For a whimsical O, use a circle cookie cutter and a smaller circle cookie cutter to create your O. Cut the small O off center.

Candy Canes

During the holidays we line the entrance to The Flour Pot with enormous display candy canes.
We then attach big, red bows to each one. These are quite a bit smaller but much tastier!

✳ ✳ ❋ ✳ ✳

WHAT YOU NEED:

Parchment paper
Fondant rolling pin
Green fondant
Leaf cookie cutter
Toothpick
White fondant
Red fondant
Candy cane cookie cutter
2 Paintbrushes
Corn syrup
Candy cane cookies
Red royal icing
Pastry bag with #2 tip
Super Pearl Luster Dust
Ribbon

DIRECTIONS:

To make the leaves, roll green fondant on parchment paper to $\frac{1}{8}$-inch thickness. Cut with your leaf cookie cutter. Use a toothpick to score veins, and a paintbrush to dust with luster dust. Set the leaves on the lip of a baking tray to create a curved shape. Let dry.

To make the candy canes, roll white fondant on parchment paper to $\frac{1}{8}$-inch thickness. With your hands, create thin ropes of red fondant and place them in a candy cane–striped pattern on the white rolled fondant. Roll with a fondant pin until smooth. Cut with your candy cane cutter. Set aside.

With a paintbrush, dab corn syrup on top of each cookie. Carefully place the fondant canes on the syrup layer, smoothing the edges with a dry finger.

With a clean brush, dust with luster dust.

With red royal icing in a pastry bag, pipe details on the candy canes.

Use additional icing to attach the leaves.

With ribbon, make a bow for each cookie. Attach with royal icing.

✳✳✳✳✳

CITY HOLIDAY

✳✳✳✳✳

Furry Friend

*Margie says: My granddog Vida is a yellow lab.
I don't think she would mind if we gussied her up for the holiday season.*

✳ ✳ ❋ ✳ ✳

WHAT YOU NEED:

Parchment paper
Fondant rolling pin
Red fondant
Dog cookie cutter
Offset spatula
2 Paintbrushes
Corn syrup
Dog cookies
Toothpick (for cuff and
collar detail)
Dog leg and dog ear
templates (page 136)
Pastry wheel or utility knife
Light yellow fondant
White royal icing
Black fondant
Gold Pearl Luster Dust
Black royal icing
Pastry bag with #2 tip
Star tip #13
Green bows (⅛-inch)

DIRECTIONS:

Roll red fondant on parchment paper to $\frac{1}{8}$-inch thickness. Cut it with your dog cookie cutter. Using an offset spatula, cut the jacket and cap shapes. Set caps aside. Dab corn syrup on top of each cookie where the jacket will rest. Place the jacket fondant on the syrup layer, smoothing the edges with a dry finger. Press a toothpick into the collar and cuff for detail.

For the leg and the ear, roll yellow fondant on parchment paper to $\frac{1}{8}$-inch thickness. Lay each template on the fondant and cut around it with a pastry wheel or utility knife. Dab corn syrup on top of each cookie where the legs and ears will attach being careful to moisten only the area that will be covered by fondant. Carefully place the fondant pieces on the syrup layer, smoothing the edges with a dry finger.

Attach the cap to each cookie, on top of the ear, with white royal icing.

For the boots, roll black fondant on parchment paper to $\frac{1}{8}$-inch thickness. Cut it with your dog cookie cutter. Use the offset spatula to cut the boots. Dab corn syrup on top of each cookie where the boots will be located. Carefully place the fondant boots on the syrup layer, smoothing the edges with a dry finger. Use a dry paintbrush to dust the fondant with luster dust.

Use black royal icing to detail the boots and the jacket belt.

Use white royal icing in a pastry bag with a star tip to pipe the cap, collar, and boot trim. Change to a #2 tip and pipe the white of the eye.

Use the black royal icing to add the pupil of the eye. Attach a green bow to the collar with additional icing. Let dry for at least one hour or until the royal icing is hardened.

Christmas in New York

Everyone should experience Christmas in New York, at least once, if they can. It really is a magical time.

✳ ✳ ✳ ✳ ✳

WHAT YOU NEED:

Parchment paper
Fondant rolling pin
Green fondant
Tree cookie cutter (for tree and taxi detail)
White royal icing
Pastry bags with #2 tip
Sanding sugar
Brown royal icing
Yellow fondant
Cab cookie cutter
Paintbrush
Corn syrup
Cab cookies
Black fondant
Circle cookie cutter
Black royal icing
Red royal Icing

DIRECTIONS:

To make the tree, roll green fondant on parchment paper to $\frac{1}{8}$-inch thickness. Cut it with your tree cookie cutter.

Pipe white royal icing to look like snow. Sprinkle the icing with white sanding sugar. Use brown royal icing to pipe the trunk. This can be made a day or so ahead of time.

To make the cab, roll yellow fondant on parchment paper to $\frac{1}{8}$-inch thickness. Cut it with your cab cookie cutter. With a paintbrush, dab corn syrup on top of each cab cookie. Place the fondant cab on the syrup layer, smoothing the edges with a dry finger.

Roll black fondant on parchment paper to $\frac{1}{8}$-inch thickness. Cut into circles with your circle cookie cutter. Using a dab of royal icing, adhere the circles to the cookies, as wheels.

With black royal icing in your pastry bag, pipe the taxi detail.

With white royal icing, pipe the checker, windshield, wheel, and headlight detail.

Use red royal icing to pipe the brake light detail.

Let dry for at least one hour or until the icing is hardened.

Use a dab of royal icing to adhere the tree to the roof of each cookie.

Tip: Black fondant is not the most mouth-friendly color, so you may want to substitute mini Oreos for the wheels if you are serving these for guests.

Christmas Balls

*Abbey says: I like Christmas-tree decorations that are clean and modern.
I love the idea of a basic color palette carried throughout the house.
These ornaments are cool and icy, perfect for a snowy Christmas Eve.*

✳ ✳ ❄ ✳ ✳

WHAT YOU NEED:

Parchment paper
Fondant rolling pin
Colored fondant
Christmas ornament
cookie cutter
3 Paintbrushes
Corn syrup
Christmas ornament cookie
Super Pearl Luster Dust
Offset spatula
Small bowl
Edible silver paint powder
Drop of vodka or lemon
extract
Dragées
White royal icing
Pastry bag with #2 tip

DIRECTIONS:

Roll colored fondant on parchment paper to $1/8$-inch thickness. Cut it with your ornament cookie cutter. Set ornaments aside.

With a paintbrush, dab corn syrup on top of each ornament cookie. Carefully place the fondant ornaments on the syrup layer, smoothing the edges with a dry finger.

Use a dry paintbrush to dust the fondant with luster dust. With the side of the offset spatula, create ridges in the neck of each ornament. Set the cookies aside.

In a small bowl, mix edible silver paint powder with a drop of vodka to make a paste. (If the paste is too thin, add more paint powder.)

Use a clean paintbrush to paint the neck of each ornament. Make sure the ridges are still visible after painting.

Dab a dot of royal icing at the top of each ornament. Adhere a dragée to the royal icing.

Another Idea: To make these real, usable ornaments, adhere a loop of ribbon under the fondant with royal icing. You can also poke a hole in the cookie before baking them; then poke a hole into the soft fondant on the cookie and tie a ribbon through both layers.

Modern Christmas Trees

Margie says: *These trees remind me of a Christmas tree that you would find in a SoHo loft.*

WHAT YOU NEED:

Parchment paper

Fondant rolling pin

Green fondant

Tree cookie cutter

Offset spatula

Paintbrush

Corn syrup

Tree cookie

Brown fondant

Hot pink fondant

Electric blue fondant

Red fondant

Various-sized pastry tips
(to use as cutters)

Pastry bag with #2 tip

Hot pink royal icing

Red royal icing

Electric blue royal icing

Lime green royal icing

Leaf green royal icing

DIRECTIONS:

Roll green fondant on parchment paper to $\frac{1}{8}$-inch thickness. Cut it with your tree cookie cutter. Cut off the trunk of each tree. With a paintbrush, dab corn syrup on tree part of each cookie. Place the green fondant on the syrup, smoothing the edges with a dry finger.

Roll brown fondant on parchment paper to $\frac{1}{8}$-inch thickness. Use your offset spatula to cut a small rectangle for the trunk. Dab corn syrup on trunk part of each cookie. Place the brown fondant on the syrup, smoothing the edges with a dry finger. Set cookies aside.

Roll the colored fondants (pink, blue, and red) and use the tops and bottoms of the pastry tips as cookie cutters to create an assortment of sizes and colors of circles. Adhere each circle with a little dab of royal icing.

With a pastry bag and a #2 tip, pipe lines of pink, red, blue, and green royal icing on the trees. Let dry for at least one hour or until the icing is hardened.

• **Abbey says:** *To get the different-sized fondant circles, we used the tops and bottoms of pastry tips as cutters. Again, this is Margie's way of thinking out of the box.*

Ballet Slippers

Abbey says: One of my fondest memories as a little girl was a special holiday treat when my mom and I spent the afternoon in town. We got dressed up and had tea at the Four Seasons; then we went to see the Nutcracker ballet.

✳ ✳ ❄ ✳ ✳

WHAT YOU NEED:

Parchment paper
Fondant rolling pin
Soft pink fondant
Ballet slipper cookie cutter
Offset spatula
2 Paintbrushes
Corn syrup
Ballet slipper cookies
Pink fondant
White fondant
Super Pearl Luster Dust
Pink royal icing
Pastry bag with #2 tip
Pastry bag with #47 tip
(basket-weave tip)
Pink ribbon

DIRECTIONS:

Roll soft pink fondant on parchment paper to $\frac{1}{8}$-inch thickness. Use your ballet slipper cookie cutter to cut the fondant. Cut the sole from each slipper. Use a paintbrush to dab corn syrup on the sole part of each cookie. Place a fondant sole on the syrup, smoothing the edges with a dry finger.

Roll the pink fondant on parchment paper to $\frac{1}{8}$-inch thickness. Cut out ballet slippers. Cut the sole and the tights from each slipper. Dab corn syrup on the middle of each cookie. Place a fondant piece on the syrup, smoothing the edges with a dry finger.

Roll white fondant on parchment paper to $\frac{1}{8}$-inch thickness. Cut out ballet slippers. Cut the sole and middle from each slipper. Dab corn syrup on top part of each cookie. Place the fondant tights on the syrup, smoothing the edges with a dry finger. With a dry paintbrush, dust the top of each cookie with luster dust.

With pink royal icing in your pastry bag, and a #2 tip, pipe the detail of each slipper.

Use a #47 tip to pipe the ribbon laces. Attach a decorative ribbon to the top right corner of each cookie.

Let the cookies dry for at least one hour or until the icing is hardened.

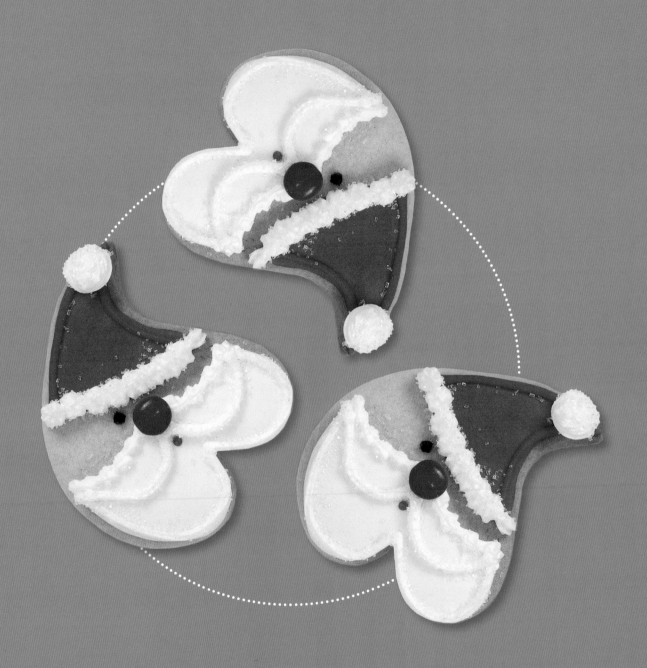

A TWINKLE
IN HIS EYE

Old St. Nick

This is our take on the lovable Old St. Nick.

✳ ✳ ✳ ✳ ✳

WHAT YOU NEED:

Parchment paper

Fondant rolling pin

Red fondant

Pennant cookie cutter
(for Santa cookies)

Offset spatula

2 Paintbrushes

Corn syrup

Santa cookies

Super Pearl Luster Dust

Black fondant

White fondant

Beard template (page 136)

White royal icing

Black royal icing

Pastry bags with #2 tip

Dragées

Pastry bag with star tip

White sanding sugar

Red royal icing

Pink Pearl Luster Dust

Pastry bag with #47 tip

DIRECTIONS:

Roll red fondant on parchment paper to $\frac{1}{8}$-inch thickness. Cut it with your pennant cookie cutter. Cut off the red jackets and caps. With a paintbrush, dab corn syrup on each Santa cookie where the cap and jacket go. Place a fondant cap and jacket on each cookie, smoothing the edges with a dry finger. Make sure there is enough space between the jacket and the cap for face detail. Dust the fondant with pearl luster dust.

Roll the black fondant on parchment paper to $\frac{1}{8}$-inch thickness. Cut feet with your pennant cookie cutter. Dab corn syrup on each cookie where the feet will go. Place the cut fondant on the syrup, smoothing the edges with a dry finger.

Roll white fondant on parchment paper to $\frac{1}{8}$-inch thickness. Cut it with your beard template. Use white royal icing and a star tip to adhere a beard to the top of each suit. Pipe the jacket and hat detail, hair, and moustache of each Santa.

With black royal icing in your pastry bag with a #2 tip, pipe an outline for the boots, belt, and the two eyes of each Santa.

Pipe the belt with black icing in a pastry bag with a #47 tip. Adhere a dragée to the royal icing, for the belt buckle.

Sprinkle with white sanding sugar.

Using red royal icing in a pastry bag with #2 tip, pipe the nose.

Use a dry paintbrush to dust the cheeks with pink luster dust.

Let the cookies dry for at least one hour or until the icing is hardened.

Dancing Santa

The fun thing about this Santa is that his separate parts give him lots of personality.

✳ ✳ ✳ ✳ ✳

WHAT YOU NEED:

Parchment paper

Fondant rolling pin

Red fondant

Light bulb cookie cutter
(for the legs)

Offset spatula

1 Paintbrush

Corn syrup

2 light bulb cookies

Santa arm template
(page 136)

2 Santa arm cookies

Green fondant

Green royal icing

Red royal icing

Pastry bag with #2 tip

White royal icing

Pastry bag with #18 star tip

White sanding sugar

Pennant cookie cutter
(for Santa cookie)

Santa cookie

DIRECTIONS:

Roll red fondant to $\frac{1}{8}$-inch thickness. Cut with the light bulb cutter. Cut the bases from the bulbs. Use a paintbrush to dab corn syrup on top of each light bulb cookie. Carefully place the red fondant bulbs on the syrup layer, smoothing the edges with a dry finger. Set the cookies aside.

Roll black fondant on parchment paper to $\frac{1}{8}$-inch thickness. Cut the fondant with the light bulb cookie cutter. Cut the bases from each bulb. Dab corn syrup on the partially finished cookies. Carefully place a fondant base on the syrup, smoothing the edges with a dry finger. Repeat for the second leg.

Using the Santa arm template repeat the above process for the arms. Instead of black fondant at the base, use green fondant. Use coordinating colors of royal icing (for example, red royal icing on red fondant) and a #2 tip to pipe outlines of the legs and arms.

Use white royal icing in a pastry bag with a star tip to pipe the seam where the black meets the red on the legs, and the green meets the red on the arms. Sprinkle white sanding sugar over the icing. Let dry one hour or until the icing is hardened.

Roll more red fondant on parchment paper to $\frac{1}{8}$-inch thickness. Cut the fondant with the pennant cookie cutter. (For a rounded waist, use your knife to shape the body.) Cut out about 1 inch of fondant from each Santa, between the cap and the suit. Dab corn syrup on top of each Santa cookie, where Santa's cap will go. Carefully place the fondant cap on the syrup, smoothing the edges with a dry finger. Repeat with Santa's suit.

Black fondant

Textured rolling pin

Knife

Red hot candies (for nose)

Black royal icing

Green M&M's

Roll black fondant on parchment paper to $\frac{1}{8}$-inch thickness. Go over once with a textured rolling pin. Use a knife to cut a thin belt. Dab a little corn syrup on each Santa cookie where the belt will go. Place the fondant belt over the syrup, smoothing the edges with a dry finger.

Using red royal icing in a pastry bag with a #2 tip, outline the suit and the cap.

Using white royal icing in a pastry bag with a star tip, create the pom-pom, cap detail, Santa's beard and face detail, and the bottom ruffle of each suit. Sprinkle white sanding sugar over the white royal icing.

Adhere a red hot to the white royal icing as Santa's nose.

Use black royal icing to pipe two dots on each cookie for eyes and to adhere a green M&M on Santa's belt.

Adhere the body to the arms and legs with royal icing to create one large cookie. Position the arms and legs to give your Santa personality.

Let dry for at least one hour or until the icing has hardened.

Santa Wedge

It's fun to use simple shapes in unusual ways.

✳ ✳ ❇ ✳ ✳

WHAT YOU NEED:

Parchment paper

Fondant rolling pin

Red fondant

Triangle cookie cutter
(for Santa cookie)

Offset spatula

Paintbrush

Corn syrup

Santa cookie

Red royal icing

Pastry bag with #2 tip

Black royal icing

White royal icing

Pastry bag with #16 tip
(star tip)

White sanding sugar

DIRECTIONS:

Roll red fondant on parchment paper to ⅛-inch thickness. Use your triangle cookie cutter to cut the fondant into triangles. Using an offset spatula, cut a thin wedge from the side of each triangle, to make a space for Santa's face. Discard the wedges. Set the cut fondant aside.

With a paintbrush, dab corn syrup on top of each cookie. Carefully place the hat and suit pieces of the red cut fondant on each cookie, smoothing the edges with a dry finger.

With red royal icing in your pastry bag, and a #2 tip, pipe Santa's nose, as well as the detail of his suit.

Use black royal icing in your pastry bag to pipe the belt and eyes. Use white royal icing to pipe Santa's moustache. Let dry for at least one hour.

With white royal icing in your pastry bag, and a #16 star tip, pipe additional suit detail and the pom-pom on each hat. Sprinkle with white sanding sugar.

Let dry for at least one hour or until the royal icing is hardened.

Santa Moon or Heart

Abbey says: These Santas remind me less of the roly-poly Santa images of today, and more of a nostalgic, almost vintage Santa. The Santa in these cookies looks refined.

✳ ✳ ❇ ✳ ✳

WHAT YOU NEED:

Parchment paper

Fondant rolling pin

White fondant

Man-in-the-Moon or Heart cookie cutter (for Santa cookie)

Utility knife

2 Paintbrushes

Corn syrup

Santa cookie

Red fondant

Pastry bag with #2 tip

Red royal icing

Pastry bag with #18 star tip

White royal icing

White sanding sugar

Black royal icing

Red M&M candy

DIRECTIONS:

Roll white fondant on parchment paper to ⅛-inch thickness. Cut the fondant with the Moon or Heart cookie cutter. Use the knife to separate the beard from the rest of each Santa. (We cut on the diagonal, as opposed to straight across, so Santa's beard is at an angle on his face.) Set the beards aside.

With a paintbrush, dab corn syrup on each cookie, where Santa's beard will go. Carefully place the fondant beards on the syrup layer, smoothing the edges with a dry finger.

Roll out the red fondant, and cut it using the Moon or Heart cookie cutter. Use the utility knife to cut away the caps. Set the caps aside.

With a paintbrush, dab corn syrup on each cookie, where the cap will rest. Attach each cap to a cookie.

With a #2 tip on your pastry bag, pipe a red royal icing outline on each cap and the mouth on the Santa Heart.

With a #18 tip on your pastry bag, pipe white royal icing stars as trim on each cap and beard. Pipe a pom-pom with the star tip. Pipe a curly moustache on Santa's face. Sprinkle some white sanding sugar on the white royal icing.

Pipe one black icing dot for an eye. Add a red M&M candy to the Santa Heart for a nose.

Let dry for at least one hour or until the icing is hardened.

NIGHT BEFORE CHRISTMAS

Not a Creature Was Stirring

Your guests are sure to stir when you put these cookies out.
Just think how much fun the cookies would be, displayed along the mantel.

❄ ❄ ❄ ❄ ❄

WHAT YOU NEED:

Parchment paper

Fondant rolling pin

Gray fondant

Ice cream cone cookie cutter
(for mouse body)

1½-inch circle cookie cutter
(for mouse ear)

1¼-inch circle cookie cutter
(for mouse ear)

Paintbrush

Corn syrup

Mouse body cookies

Mouse ear cookies

Pink fondant

Gray royal icing

Pastry bags with #2 tip

White royal icing

Black royal icing

Toothpicks

Red candy (for example,
gumballs)

Ribbon

Shoestring licorice

DIRECTIONS:

Roll gray fondant on parchment paper to $\frac{1}{8}$-inch thickness. Cut it into shapes with your mouse body cookie cutter and the two circles (two of each size circle, per mouse). Use a paintbrush to dab corn syrup on the tops of your mouse body and ear cookies. Place the fondant on the syrup layer of the corresponding cookie, smoothing the edges with a dry finger. Set cookies aside.

Roll pink fondant on parchment paper to $\frac{1}{8}$-inch thickness. Cut it with your circle cookie cutter. Use royal icing to adhere the pink fondant to the gray fondant circles to look like the insides of the ears.

With gray royal icing in a pastry bag with a #2 tip, pipe the outline of each mouse body and outline the ears. Use additional royal icing to adhere the ears to the body.

Using white royal icing, pipe two small ovals on each mouse's head, for the whites of the eyes. With another pastry bag filled with black royal icing, pipe two round dots for the eyeballs.

Adhere the toothpicks with additional royal icing, to make whiskers. Use dots of royal icing to add a red candy nose, a bow, and a licorice tail to each cookie.

Let dry for at least one hour or until the icing is hardened.

Dimensional Tree

Abbey says: We had been working on the design of the dimensional tree for what seemed like forever. It just felt like something was missing. Then, Jackie, one of our cookie decorators, suggested spun sugar. The result was absolutely stunning.

✳ ✳ ❄ ✳ ❄

WHAT YOU NEED:

White fondant
Parchment paper
Fondant rolling pin
Tree cookie cutter
Utility knife
2 Paintbrushes
Corn syrup
3 tree cookies cut in half vertically to create 6 pieces*
Super Pearl Luster Dust
Pretzel rod
White royal icing
Pastry bag with #2 tip
Gold dragées
Spun sugar (page 134)

*Make sure to cut the trunk off of the tree before you bake it. Use a knife or offset spatula, so you will get a clean cut.

DIRECTIONS:

Create a 1-inch ball of white fondant in the palm of your hand. Set aside.

Roll white fondant on parchment paper to $\frac{1}{8}$-inch thickness. Cut three fondant trees with your cookie cutter. Use a knife to cut off the tree trunks and to cut the fondant in half vertically to match the baked cookie pieces. Set fondant aside.

Using a paintbrush, dab corn syrup on each cookie piece. Carefully place the coordinating fondant pieces on the syrup layer, smoothing the edges with a dry finger. Repeat for all six cookie pieces. Use a dry paintbrush to dust with luster dust. Let dry for at least one hour or until hardened.

Turn the cookie pieces over, so the fondant sides are down, and repeat the above fondant process for the backs of the cookies. Again, dust with luster dust and let the cookies dry one hour. To assemble the tree, start with two cookie pieces and the pretzel rod. Use white royal icing to adhere the straight edges of the tree to the pretzel rod. The pretzel will act as the anchor. Repeat until all the pieces are adhered. Carefully stand the tree up, propping it with a mug or other kitchen item, and let dry for at least one hour or until the icing is completely hardened.

Using royal icing in a pastry bag and a #2 tip, adhere the reserved fondant ball to the top of the tree. Use additional icing to attach the gold dragées to the tree.

Let dry for at least one hour or until the icing is hardened. Wrap with spun sugar.

Tip: Spun sugar has a tendency to wilt. Add just before presenting the cookie.

Toasty PJ's

Our head "piper," Sandy, has a tradition of giving everyone in the family pajamas on Christmas Eve. It started when her mom came to spend the night on Christmas Eve, but didn't have anything fun to wear.

✳ ✳ ✳ ✳ ✳

WHAT YOU NEED:

Parchment paper
Fondant rolling pin
Green fondant
White fondant
Shirt cookie cutter
Pant cookie cutter
Paintbrush
Corn syrup
Shirt cookie (for pajama top)
Pant cookie (for pajama bottom)
White royal icing
Pastry bag with #2 tip
Red bows
Offset spatula
Red fondant

DIRECTIONS:

Roll green fondant on parchment paper to $1/8$-inch thickness. Set aside.

Make thin ropes of white fondant. Place the ropes on the green rolled fondant, and roll with a rolling pin until smooth. Cut it with your shirt and pant cookie cutters. With a paintbrush, dab corn syrup on top of each cookie. Carefully place the fondant pieces on the syrup, smoothing the edges with a dry finger.

With white royal icing in your pastry bag, pipe detail on the pajamas. Adhere a small bow to the icing. Let dry for at least one hour or until the fondant is hardened.

Repeat the process with red fondant and pea-sized balls of white fondant rolled into it to make different kinds of pajamas.

To create pajamas with a collar, roll green fondant on parchment paper to $1/8$-inch thickness. Make thin ropes of white fondant. Place the ropes on the green fondant and roll with a rolling pin. Cut it with your shirt cookie cutter. Cut off the top of each shirt top (where the collar will go). Dab corn syrup on top of each cookie where the collar will go. Place the fondant on the syrup, smoothing the edges with a dry finger.

• **Margie says:** The #2 tip lends a delicate, lacelike look to the pajama detail.

Dancing Reindeer

Abbey says: *We started making dimensional cookies sometime back for an event with a farm-animal theme. I think they are so silly, because they have a puppetlike quality.*

✳ ✳ ❋ ✳ ✳

WHAT YOU NEED:

Parchment paper
Fondant rolling pin
Chocolate fondant
Brown fondant
Reindeer cookie cutter
Offset spatula
Paintbrush
Corn syrup
Reindeer cookies (bodies only; cut off the heads, leaving a little neck)
Small gingerbread man cookie cutter
Small gingerbread man cookies (for reindeer head)
Brown royal icing
Pastry bag with #2 tip
Green royal icing
Pastry bag with leaf tip #352
Red royal icing
White royal icing
Black royal icing
Red M&M's

DIRECTIONS:

Roll chocolate and brown fondant together with your hands just until marbled, two-tone effect achieved. Roll the mixed fondant on parchment paper to $1/8$-inch thickness. Cut the fondant with your reindeer cookie cutter. Cut off the heads, leaving a little of the neck. With a paintbrush, dab corn syrup on the body of each reindeer cookie. Carefully place the fondant reindeer bodies on the syrup, smoothing the edges with a dry finger.

Roll out more of the marbled fondant to $1/8$-inch thickness. Cut with the gingerbread man cookie cutter. Dab corn syrup on top of each small gingerbread man cookie. Place the fondant pieces on top of the syrup, smoothing the edges with a dry finger.

Turn the gingerbread cookie upside down and adhere to the reindeer's neck with a dab of icing. Repeat with the remaining cookies.

With brown icing in your pastry bag, pipe the outline of each reindeer's body and the antlers on the reindeer's head.

To decorate the head, pipe a leaf below each pair of antlers using green icing in the pastry bag with a leaf tip.

Use red icing and a #2 tip to pipe holly berries on the leaves.

With white icing, pipe the eyes, and finish the eyes with a dot of black icing. Use additional icing to adhere a red M&M for the nose.

Let dry for at least one hour or until the icing is hardened.

✳✳✳✳✳
SANTA'S WORKSHOP
✳✳✳✳✳

North Pole Sign

This worn-looking North Pole directional sign looks as if little elves made it.

✳ ✳ ❋ ✳ ✳

WHAT YOU NEED:

Green fondant

Lollipop stick

2 Paintbrushes

Super Pearl Luster Dust

Red ribbon

White royal icing

Parchment paper

Fondant rolling pin

White fondant

Rectangle cookie cutter

Corn syrup

3 Cookies (with one end cut like an arrow) baked on 1 lollipop stick

Utility knife

Pastry bag with #18 star tip

Sugar holly leaf and holly

Bow

White sanding sugar

Green or red royal icing

Pastry bag with #2 tip

DIRECTIONS:

With a little luster dust in your hands, roll a three-quarter-inch ball of green fondant. Use a lollipop stick to poke a hole in the ball. Remove the stick. Set aside.

Wrap red ribbon around the stem of the lollipop stick. Use white royal icing to adhere the ribbon to the top and bottom of the stick. Slide the stick into the hole that you created earlier in the fondant ball. Secure with royal icing.

Roll white fondant on parchment paper to $\frac{1}{8}$-inch thickness. Cut the fondant with your cookie cutter, near the rough edge of the fondant. This will give a ragged look to the fondant. With a knife cut one end to look like an arrow. With a paintbrush, dab a little corn syrup on each cookie. Place the fondant on the syrup layer, smoothing the edges with a dry finger. Repeat for all cookies. Use a dry paintbrush to dust with luster dust.

With a #18 tip on your pastry bag, pipe white royal icing as snow on the signs.

Adhere a sugar holly leaf and a bow to the icing. Sprinkle the icing with white sanding sugar.

Use red or green royal icing in your pastry bag, with a #2 tip, to pipe fun road names.

Let dry for at least one hour or until the icing is hardened.

Tip: Secure the cookies to the lollipop stick with some royal icing. Let dry.

Elf Boot

The gold balls on these boots add dimension, and you can almost hear them jingle as the little elves assemble toys for the big day.

✳ ✳ ❆ ✳ ✳

WHAT YOU NEED:

Edible gold powder

White fondant

Parchment paper

Fondant rolling pin

Leaf green fondant

Red fondant (for integrating with green, and for boot tops)

Elf boot cookie cutter

Christmas tree cookie cutter

Oval cookie cutter

2 Paintbrushes

Corn syrup

Elf boot cookies

Electric green fondant

Super Pearl Luster Dust

Electric green royal icing

Pastry bag with #2 tip

Red royal icing

DIRECTIONS:

To create gold ball details, place a dab of edible gold powder in the palm of your hand. Then roll white fondant into small balls to cover completely in gold. Add gold powder as needed. Set aside.

For stockings, roll leaf green fondant on parchment paper to $\frac{1}{8}$-inch thickness. Then create small balls of red fondant. Place them on the rolled green fondant; roll with a rolling pin to integrate. Cut into boot shapes with elf boot cookie cutter.

Use the side of your Christmas tree cookie cutter to cut off the bottom of each boot. Use an oval cookie cutter to cut into the heel of each boot. Discard the heel cutouts and the tops of the boots. Set the remaining fondant pieces aside.

With a paintbrush, dab corn syrup on top of each cookie. Carefully place the fondant on the syrup layer, smoothing the edges with a dry finger. Set aside.

Roll electric green fondant on parchment paper to $\frac{1}{8}$-inch thickness. Again, cut with your elf boot cookie cutter. Use the side of your Christmas tree cutter to cut the bottoms of the boots, keeping in mind where they will fit into the leaf green fondant. Use the oval cutter to cut into the heels. Set aside.

Dab corn syrup on the middle and at the heel of each cookie. Place the fondant pieces on the syrup layer; smooth the edges with a dry finger. Repeat with red fondant for the top of each boot. Use a dry paintbrush and dust with luster dust.

With electric green royal icing in your pastry bag, pipe detail on each boot. With red royal icing, pipe detail on the top of each boot and adhere the gold balls. Let dry.

Gingerbread Rudolph

See recipe for Gingerbread Cookie Dough on page 127.

✳ ✳ ❋ ✳ ✳

WHAT YOU NEED:

Parchment paper

Fondant rolling pin

Brown fondant

Teardrop cookie cutter
(1-inch long)

Ball tool

Foam pad (for using ball
tool on ears)

Pastry bags with #2 tip

Brown royal icing

Gingerbread Rudolph cookie

Sugar leaves (store-bought)

Red candies

Black royal icing

White royal icing

Pennant cookie cutter
(for Rudolph cookie)

1 Paintbrush

DIRECTIONS:

To make the ears, roll brown fondant on parchment paper to ⅛-inch thickness. Cut with your teardrop cookie cutter, two ears for each reindeer. With the fondant teardrop on the foam pad, gently use a ball tool in a circular motion in the center of the teardrop to create a bowl shape. Don't press too hard or you will go through the fondant. Let harden. Set aside.

To decorate the cookie, pipe antlers on each reindeer cookie using brown royal icing in your pastry bag with a #2 tip.

Adhere the ears with royal icing. Use additional icing to attach the sugar leaves, overlapping on the ears, and to adhere the candy nose. (We used a nonpareil.)

Use white royal icing to create the base of each eye.

Use black royal icing to complete the eye. Finish with brown eyebrows, using brown royal icing in your pastry bag.

Let dry for at least one hour or until the icing is hardened.

Another idea: We used nonpareils for the nose, but any red candy will work: M&M's, gumballs, you name it. If you don't have candy, use a ball of red fondant.

Tip: Pipe eyes with personality! The placement of the pupil can give the reindeer different personalities. Play around with some eyes on the parchment before you pipe on the cookie.

North Pole Express (Caboose)

What Christmas tree is complete without a toy train running around its base?

✳ ✳ ❄ ✳ ✳

WHAT YOU NEED:

Parchment paper
Fondant rolling pin
Red fondant
White fondant
Caboose cookie cutter
Offset spatula
1 Paintbrush
Corn syrup
Caboose cookie
Green fondant
Circle cookie cutter
Red royal icing
Necco wafers
(2 per cookie)
Gumdrops
Pastry bag with #2 tip
White royal icing
White sanding sugar
Green royal icing
Black royal icing

DIRECTIONS:

For the caboose body, roll red fondant on parchment paper to $\frac{1}{8}$-inch thickness. To create dots, roll pea-sized balls of white fondant in your hands and place them on the red fondant. Roll with a rolling pin until the white balls are incorporated into the red. Cut the fondant with your cookie cutter. Use the offset spatula to cut off the top and the back of each caboose. Discard these smaller pieces. Set the remaining piece aside.

With a dry paintbrush, paint corn syrup on each cookie. Carefully place the fondant on the syrup layer, smoothing the edges with a dry finger. Set the cookies aside.

Roll green fondant on parchment paper to $\frac{1}{8}$-inch thickness. Cut the fondant with your cookie cutter. Again, use the offset spatula to cut off the top and back of each caboose. Discard the large pieces.

Using the remaining, small pieces of green fondant, adhere them with corn syrup to the exposed parts of each cookie. Set the cookies aside.

For the caboose sign, roll red fondant on parchment paper to $\frac{1}{8}$-inch thickness. Use a quarter-sized circle cookie cutter to cut the fondant into circles. Use a dab of red royal icing to place a circle on the top of each caboose.

For the wheels, use red royal icing to adhere two Necco wafers to each cookie. Use royal icing to add gum drops to the wheels.

For the detail, use white royal icing in a pastry bag with a #2 tip to create snow and other caboose detail. Sprinkle white sanding sugar on the wet icing. Use green, red, and black royal icing to personalize your train and give it character.

North Pole Express (Toy Car)

✳ ✳ ❋ ✳ ✳

WHAT YOU NEED:

Parchment paper

Fondant rolling pin

Small assortment of colored
fondants

Assorted 1½-inch cookie
cutters (for toys)

Assorted colors of royal icing,
for toy detail and placement

Green fondant

White fondant

Caboose cookie cutter

Offset spatula

1 Paintbrush

Corn syrup

Caboose cookie (with the top
cut straight across)

Red fondant

Necco wafers (2 per car)

Gumdrops (2 per car)

White royal icing

Pastry bag with #2 tip

White sanding sugar

Green royal icing

Red royal icing

Black royal icing

DIRECTIONS:

To make the toys, roll assorted colors of fondant on parchment paper to ⅛-inch thickness. Cut into various toy shapes using your mini cookie cutters. Pipe the details with royal icing. Let dry for at least one hour or until the icing is hardened. These can be made a day or so ahead of time.

To make the toy car body, roll green fondant on parchment paper to ⅛-inch thickness. To create stripes, use your hands to roll white fondant into thin ropes. Place them on the green fondant. Roll with a rolling pin until the white ropes are incorporated into the green. Cut the striped fondant with your caboose cookie cutter. Use the offset spatula to separate the top, front, and back from each car. Discard these three smaller pieces. Set toy car aside.

Use a dry paintbrush to paint corn syrup on each cookie, being careful to leave the top of each toy car unpainted. (This is where the toys will go.) Carefully place the fondant on the syrup layer, smoothing the edges with a dry finger. Set the cookies aside.

On fresh parchment paper, roll red fondant to ⅛-inch thickness. Cut the fondant with your cookie cutter. Again, use the offset spatula to separate the front and back from each toy car. Using only these small pieces, adhere them with corn syrup to the exposed parts of each cookie.

For toy placement, use corresponding colors of royal icing to attach your premade fondant toy shapes, in a whimsical configuration, to the top of each boxcar. Hold the toys in place or prop them up until they are secure.

For the wheels, use royal icing to adhere two Necco wafers to each cookie. Use additional royal icing to add gumdrops to the wheels.

To decorate: Use white royal icing in a pastry bag to create snow and detail on each boxcar. Sprinkle white sanding sugar on the wet icing.

North Pole Express (Engine)

✳ ✳ ❊ ✳ ✳

WHAT YOU NEED:

Parchment paper

Fondant rolling pin

Red fondant

Green fondant

White fondant

Engine cookie cutter

Offset spatula

1 paintbrush

Corn syrup

Engine cookie

2 Circle cookie cutters
(different sizes)

Red royal icing

Black royal icing

Green royal icing

Pastry bag with #2 tip

Pastry bag with
basket-weave tip

Necco wafers (3 per cookie)

Gum drops

White sanding sugar

DIRECTIONS:

For the engine body, roll red fondant on parchment paper to $\frac{1}{8}$-inch thickness. Cut the fondant with your cookie cutter. Use the offset spatula to cut off the front headlight and front and back of the engine (in the picture these parts are white and green). Discard the smaller pieces. Dab corn syrup on each cookie. Carefully place the fondant on the syrup layer, smoothing edges with a dry finger. Set the cookies aside.

Roll green fondant on parchment paper to $\frac{1}{8}$-inch thickness. Cut the fondant with your engine cookie cutter. Again, use the offset spatula to cut off the front and back detail of the engine. Adhere the small front and end pieces of green fondant with corn syrup to the exposed parts of each cookie. Set the cookies aside.

Repeat with white fondant for the headlight.

For the large wheel, roll white fondant on parchment paper to $\frac{1}{8}$-inch thickness. Create thin ropes with red fondant and green fondant. Place ropes on white fondant and use a rolling pin to incorporate into the white fondant to create stripes on the wheel. Cut with large circle cutter. Adhere to the train cookie using royal icing.

For the small wheels, use royal icing to adhere Necco wafers to the cookie. Use red royal icing to add gum drops and pipe the connector between the gum drops.

For the window, roll green fondant on parchment paper to $\frac{1}{8}$-inch thickness. Cut the fondant with your small circle cookie cutter. Use royal icing to adhere the fondant.

To create the Santa belt train on top of the train use black royal icing in a pastry bag with a basket-weave tip.

For the other detail, use white royal icing in a pastry bag with a #2 tip to create snow and other engine detail. Sprinkle white sanding sugar on the wet icing. Use green, red, and black royal icing to personalize your train.

✳✳✳✳✳

BASICS

✳✳✳✳✳

Cookie Dough

There's no smell quite like a kitchen full of fresh baked cookies.

✳ ✳ ❋ ✳ ✳

Yields 3 to 4 dozen (3½-inch) cookies

WHAT YOU NEED:

3 cups (1 pound) all-
purpose flour
1 teaspoon baking powder
½ pound (2 sticks)
unsalted butter,
room temperature
1 cup granulated sugar
1 large egg, room
temperature
1 teaspoon pure
vanilla extract
Parchment paper

DIRECTIONS:

Preheat the oven to 350°F.

Sift the flour and the baking powder together in a bowl. In an electric mixing bowl using the paddle attachment, cream the butter and sugar, about 3 minutes. Add the egg and vanilla and beat another minute or so. Add the flour mixture in two batches and beat until the dough begins to pull away from the sides of the bowl.

Transfer the dough to a piece of parchment paper. Using your hands, knead the dough for about a minute. Place the dough in a plastic bag and refrigerate for at least an hour to make it easier to handle when you begin to roll it out. However, if you must, you can roll the cookies immediately without refrigeration.

Roll the dough with a rolling pin until it is about ⅛-inch thick. (We roll our cookies on parchment paper so there is no need for extra flour.) When they bake, these cookies will not really spread, so you can place them pretty close to each other on a baking tray. If you are creating a cookie on a stick, this is the time to place lollipop sticks in your cookies.

Bake for 8 minutes or until the cookies begin to take on a golden color. They will continue to cook when removed from the oven, so don't let them get too brown before taking them out. These cookies also freeze well, but don't freeze the cookies once they are decorated. To give them that just-baked taste, pop them back in the oven for a minute or two.

Gingerbread Cookie Dough

Margie says: This is great for rolled cookie shapes and gingerbread houses.

Yield about 3 dozen 4-inch cookies

WHAT YOU NEED:

4 cups unbleached all-purpose flour

½ teaspoon baking soda

1 teaspoon salt

1 tablespoon ground cinnamon

1 teaspoon ground nutmeg

1½ tablespoons ground ginger

1 teaspoon ground cloves

½ pound (2 sticks) cold unsalted butter

⅔ cup light brown sugar

⅔ cup unsulfured molasses

2 large eggs, at room temperature

DIRECTIONS:

Combine all dry ingredients (flour to cloves) in a large mixing bowl and whisk together. Set aside.

In a separate bowl, combine the butter, brown sugar, and molasses. Using the paddle attachment of an electric mixer beat on medium speed. Scrape down the sides and continue to beat until smooth and creamy. Add the eggs one at a time, beating and scraping the sides of the bowl after each addition.

With the mixer on low, carefully add the dry ingredients to the butter mixture, mixing until just combined.

Turn the dough onto parchment paper, shaping it into a workable ball. Divide the ball in half and wrap in plastic wrap or plastic bags. Refrigerate for one hour or, preferably, overnight.

Once dough is well chilled, preheat the oven to 350°F. Using a scant amount of flour, roll the dough on parchment paper to about ¼-inch thickness. Cut into desired shapes with cookie cutters. Re-roll scraps as needed keeping the remaining dough in the refrigerator.

Place the unbaked cookies onto a baking sheet and bake for 10 minutes.

Tip: It is important to roll the dough quickly as it has a tendency to get very sticky. Resist the urge to add more flour or the result will be a tough cookie.

Chocolate Cookie Dough

Margie says: My mom used to make a Yule log out of store-bought thin chocolate wafers and whipped cream. The thin chocolate cookies were dark and very rich, and I used to eat them out of the box as fast as she was lining them up with the whipped cream. These cookies remind me of that taste. They certainly stand on their own, but they are also delicious as a cookie sandwich.

❇ ❇ ❇ ❇ ❇

Yields 3 to 4 dozen (3½-inch) cookies

WHAT YOU NEED:

1½ cups all-purpose flour

½ cup plus 2 tablespoons dark cocoa

⅛ teaspoon salt

1½ sticks unsalted butter, at room temperature

1½ cups sifted confectioners' sugar

1 large egg

¾ teaspoon pure vanilla extract

*I liked the blend of cocoas in the Hershey's brand.

DIRECTIONS:

Sift the flour, cocoa powder, and salt in a bowl.

In the bowl of an electric mixer, combine the butter and confectioners' sugar and beat on medium-high speed until pale and fluffy.

Add the egg and vanilla. Reduce the speed to low and gradually add the flour mixture. Continue to beat until well combined and the dough is pulling away from the sides. Wrap the dough in plastic wrap and refrigerate until firm, about 1 hour.

Preheat oven to 350°F.

Roll the dough on lightly floured parchment paper to about ⅛-inch thick. Cut with your favorite cutter. Transfer the shapes to a parchment paper–lined baking sheet, spacing the cookies 2 inches apart. Bake for about 8 minutes, until crisp. Let cool.

Tip: While rolling, keep the portion of the dough that you are not using in the refrigerator. This dough gets soft with too much handling, so you must work quickly. These cookies freeze well.

Chocolate Chip Shortbread Cookie Dough

Margie says: I weighed the ingredients for this recipe because I wanted to be exact with the powdered sugar. A great investment in baking is a digital scale. That way your measurements are always the same.

Yields 15 (3½-inch) cookies

WHAT YOU NEED:

3½ cups all-purpose flour

Pinch of salt

1 pound (4 sticks) unsalted butter, at room temperature

1 (8-ounce) box confectioners' sugar

2 teaspoons pure vanilla extract

16 ounces mini semisweet chocolate chips

DIRECTIONS:

Preheat the oven to 350°F.

Combine the flour and salt in a bowl and set aside.

Sift the confectioners' sugar into the bowl of an electric mixer. With the mixer on low to medium speed, beat in the butter until light and fluffy.

Add the vanilla and mix well.

With mixer on low speed, add the flour mixture and beat until well blended. Add the chocolate chips and mix until just combined. Wrap in plastic wrap and refrigerate.

On parchment paper, roll the cookie dough to ⅛-inch thickness, using a small bit of dough at a time. Cut with your favorite cutter*. Transfer the cookies to a parchment paper–lined baking sheet and bake for 8 minutes.

Tip: Because these cookies have chocolate chips, use a sharp metal cutter to cut through the chips. Plastic cutters do not work as well.

Variation: *To make a chocolate chocolate chip shortbread, add 1 tablespoon cocoa to the flour in the above directions. These cookies freeze well.*

✳ ✳ Fondant ✳ ✳

ONDANT IS TRADITIONALLY used on cakes, but we like to use it on our cookies for an elegant effect. In our workshops, we tell people that rolled fondant is like an edible, grown-up version of clay. It's pliable, can be colored, and dries in whatever shapes and forms you mold it into. Ready-made fondant is available in several sizes, from 1½-pound packets to 15-pound buckets. We buy white fondant and chocolate-flavored fondant. Whenever we need colored fondant, we use gel paste to mix the colors ourselves.

Warming fondant in your hands before rolling—it's more pliable.

Fondant has a long shelf life. The manufacturers say six months, but we use it so quickly, we've never had to store it that long. However, if you do purchase ready-made fondant, remember that it should not be refrigerated or frozen. We don't freeze decorated cookies either, but I have been told by some loyal customers that if you cover the decorated cookies with plastic wrap and freeze them in an airtight container, the cookies will be okay. Just make sure, when defrosting them, that the condensation is on the plastic wrap and not the cookie.

Fondant is air-sensitive. It is necessary to store fondant in an airtight container or plastic bags with zipper closings. Only take out what you're using or it will begin to dry out.

When using the fondant, warm it up in your hands and roll into a ball shape before rolling it out.

Fondant can be temperamental. It is more difficult to work with in humidity and takes longer to dry. If fondant is too sticky and not rolling properly, add a little bit of corn starch to the fondant.

Fondant is easiest to roll out on parchment paper.

COLORING FONDANT

Remember: Colors are for fun! They don't have to be realistic. We use many colors in our decorations— the more the better! And we don't even bother to match them because we feel they're more whimsical when they're colorful.

The best thing to do when coloring fondant

When making colored fondant, use color sparingly at first. It's always easier to add color than to take it away!

Kneading warms fondant and incorporates the added color.

is to work in small batches. This can be a messy process. We recommend wearing latex gloves if you do not want to get dye on your hands.

Start with a 5-inch ball of fondant and knead it in your hands a bit. It will become pliable and ready to roll or mold into whatever shape you desire. It is at this time we add the dye.

We use gel paste as opposed to liquid food coloring to dye our fondant. Gel paste is very concentrated, so you need very little to get a good colored fondant. Start with two small drops and knead. Add more coloring to achieve the desired color.

Remember, it is always easier to add more color. If the color becomes too dark, take a bit of the colored fondant and add that to a larger piece of white fondant. Don't add white to the large colored piece or you will create a lot of wasted fondant.

Dying dark colors requires quite a bit of gel paste kneaded into the fondant. We find that black and purple dyes leave a bit of an aftertaste, so we try to use chocolate fondant instead.

If your project requires many colors of fondant, we suggest making all of the batches of colors at one time. That way, you do not have to stop and start in the midst of creating the cookies. It's like having all of your ingredients ready before preparing a meal.

There are two ways to blend colors of fondant:

• Drop dots of two colors of gel paste into the fondant and mix until you achieve your desired color. Ex: blue + yellow = green.

• Use an equal part of already rolled blue fondant with already rolled yellow and knead it together. Voila! It's green!

Part of the fun is seeing the colors you can create. We work basically with the same palette of colors—soft pinks, greens, blues, yellows, etc. We also use bright tones of these colors. We stay away from colors like maroon or royal blue because they do not seem as appetizing!

Make sure you store the colors in separate airtight baggies.

PATTERNED FONDANT

It's also fun to make designs in fondant as you roll it. Some ideas for creating designs include:

Dots

Let's say you want blue dots on pink fondant. First, make blue fondant. Then make pink fondant. Roll the pink fondant until it is a bit thicker than you want. Make pea-sized balls of blue fondant with your hands. Place the balls on

the pink fondant and roll again. Roll in different ways so the dots don't totally lose their shape. Your dots will incorporate into the main piece of fondant, creating pink fondant with blue dots!

Lines

Lines are created in the fondant the same way as dots. Instead of rolling pea-sized balls of fondant, roll thin, snake-like ropes and place them on a rolled piece of fondant. Cross snakes to make zig zags, and use different colors to make plaids.

Striation

We use a lot of color striation. The cookies don't look as flat ,and they seem to have more depth and interest. By just kneading white fondant into any bit of colored fondant, various patters will appear. You can roll the fondant at this point and see what designs you create!

Keep in mind that fondant can turn murky from rolling contrasting color combinations together. Try to use colors that, when combined, will create another color. Ex: Blue dots on pink base kneaded together will turn purple.

Roll fondant dots in all ways, so they don't lose their shape.

Placing fondant ropes for making striped fondant.

Rolling ropes into the fondant.

Meringue Powder Royal Icing

Traditionally, royal icing is made using egg whites.
However, this can be unsafe because the egg whites are uncooked.
Royal icing made with meringue powder does away with this concern.

WHAT YOU NEED:

1/4 cup meringue powder

1/2 cup cold water

1 pound 10X powdered sugar

DIRECTIONS:

Combine the meringue powder, water, and sugar in the bowl of a stand mixer. Begin on low speed to moisten the powdered sugar. Increase the speed to high and beat for 5 minutes or until stiff peaks form. You should be able to hold the icing onto a spoon without it dripping off.

This icing will keep for up to three days in an airtight container. No refrigeration is needed.

Spun Sugar

Be very careful when working with sugar. This is not an activity for kids.
Sugar burns can be very dangerous and are not easy to treat.
But if done safely and correctly, the result is dramatic.

WHAT YOU NEED:

2 cups granulated sugar

½ cup water (just enough to
wet the sugar)

DIRECTIONS:

Pour the sugar into a medium saucepan. Add the water, stirring with a wooden spoon. Make sure all the sugar is submerged. Turn the heat on high, but do not stir or touch the mixture. (This is when the crystallization happens. If sugar crumbs appear on surface, the process will not work, and you will have to start over.)

When the mixture starts to boil, pay attention to the color. When it reaches a golden brown, remove the pan from the heat and place it directly into an ice-water bath for 5 seconds.

Using only one hand, dip two forks into the sugar mixture, and raise the forks together as high as you can in the air so that long strands of sugar are formed but do not break. Working over parchment paper, with your opposite hand, begin pulling the sugar off of the forks to create a tumbleweed of sugar—known as *spun sugar*. (Note: As you're pulling the sugar, watch for clumps. If clumps form, do not touch them. They will still be hot!) Use the spun sugar to decorate your cookies.

Tip: It is very important that all of your tools in this process are very clean. To loosen the sugar mixture if it gets stiff as you are working with it, place the pot on low heat and then repeat the cooking process.

❋ ❋ Piping and Supplies ❋ ❋

MARGIE SAYS: When I have an order of many cookies and have to pipe repeatedly, I go into what Abbey calls the "piping zone." A rhythm develops and the movement of my hand results in an even flow along the cookies. Swirls are almost musical, like lines waltzing across the pan of cookies. Dots are like little staccato notes that jump across the cookies!

Piping must be relaxed. Allow your hand to dance across the cookies. Before you pipe onto cookies, practice piping lines and dots onto parchment paper. Try angling the pastry bag in different ways to see how different line widths can be formed. Draw lots of lines randomly and just let your hand follow the lines with the piping bag.

When I first began using the piping bag, I was nervous about making mistakes, so I only used white icing. I could always "erase" it if necessary. White is a lot more forgiving than other colors, which makes it a good practice color. When it's still wet, you can just wipe the icing off. If you make a mistake with other colors, it is best to let the icing totally dry and then pick it off gently with a toothpick. Then proceed back over the same line.

You can find pastry bags and tips at your local grocery store, specialty cooking stores, or craft stores.

When you're ready to pipe, fill the pastry bag only halfway, as a full bag will result in icing coming out of the top of the bag and making a mess. Release any air from the top of your pastry bag before twisting it at the top to keep icing from spilling out. Hold the bag in your writing hand and guide it with your other hand.

SINCE OUR FIRST BOOK, we have had countless questions about fondant. I can't stress this point enough: not all fondant is created equal. The fondant we use is a wonderfully sweet-tasting icing, without a bitter aftertaste. I would highly recommend sourcing your fondant from a bakery. We even sell it on our Web site www.flourpotcookies.com.

Many of the decorating supplies and cookie cutters used in this book can also be found on our Web site www.flourpotcookies.com.

✳ ✳ Templates ✳ ✳

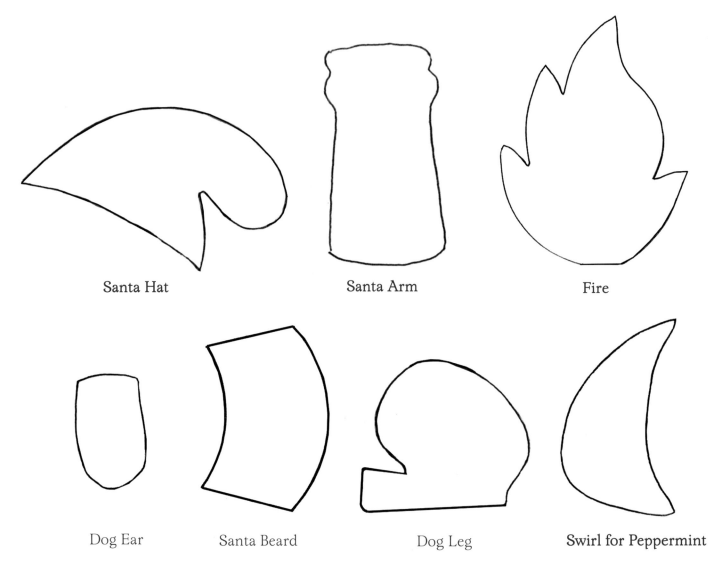

Santa Hat

Santa Arm

Fire

Dog Ear

Santa Beard

Dog Leg

Swirl for Peppermint